CHINA'S
SUPER
CONSUMERS

CHINA'S
SUPER
CONSUMERS

**WHAT 1 BILLION CUSTOMERS WANT
AND HOW TO SELL IT TO THEM**

SAVIO CHAN AND MICHAEL ZAKKOUR

WILEY

For my parents, Hal and Cynthia, for their unconditional love and who, from the beginning, gave me the gift of curiosity, a love for history, a global outlook, and belief in the potential and promise of my life—and for my wife, Monique, and son, Julian, who have fulfilled that promise.

—Michael

To my mother and father, and grandmother. For always believing in me. To my daughter, Kristi, who is my inspiration.

—Savio

CONTENTS

Preface   *xi*
Acknowledgments   *xiii*

Introduction: The China Dream   1
      Our Intent   7
      The Country within a Country   7

PART I   **History, Culture, and Language
Matter—The Birth of Chinese
Consumerism**   **11**

Chapter 1   From Feudalism to Fendi   13
      Back to the Future   14
      *Chinese Consumption: What's Old Is New Again
        (Tenfold!)*   16
      China's Growth Is Different   18

Chapter 2   Orientation   21
      A Code to the Chinese Mind-set   24
      Contradiction and Paradox   30
      Summary   31

Chapter 3   A Self-Contained Empire   33

Chapter 4   The First Globalization   41

Chapter 5   Marco Polo and the Two Admirals of the Sea   43
      The Two Admirals of the Sea   44

Chapter 6   An Insatiable Appetite   49
      Freedom Creates Wealth in the West   51

Chapter 7   Opium, Imperialism, and Decay   53
                Opium and War   54
                A Century of Exploitation   54
                End of War—Continuation of War   56

Chapter 8   The People's Republic   57
                The New China   58

Chapter 9   The Mandate of Heaven   61
                Opening and Reform   65
                Green Shoots   67

Chapter 10 A Boom Is Born   69
                A Boom Starts with a Swoosh and a Shot
                    of Espresso   71
                Change at Hyper Speed   74

PART II   **The Chinese Super Consumer—From**
                Birth to Adolescence and Maturity   **77**

Chapter 11 From Sandpaper to Sephora—The First Super
                Consumers   79
                American Century Redux   80
                Want. Need. Buy. Show Off. Keep Up.   82
                Super Consumption Goes Global   82
                Go West, Young Man   83
                China's Own Postwar Boom and Birth of the Chinese
                    Super Consumer   85
                In the Beginning   87

Chapter 12 The China Market + The China Global
                Demographic = China's Super Consumers   91
                The China Whisperer   93
                Spinning in a Whirlpool   95
                The Great Pizza Wars: In China, Everything Is
                    Possible, but Nothing Is Easy   96
                Listen to the Great One   97
                Stay the Course, Even When the Seas Get Rough 98
                Nestlé: Navigating the Teen Years   100

Chapter 13 The China Global Demographic   103
                The Precious Gift of Time   104
                Meet the Tangs   107

Chapter 14 Channels 113
    Department Stores 114
    Street-Level Stores 115
    Malls 116
    Grocery Stores/Supermarkets 118
    Hypermarkets 119
    Convenience Stores 120
    Not Your Father's Post Office 121
    Lifestyle Stores 126
    Specialty Retailers 127
    Multibrand Retail 127

Chapter 15 E-commerce and the Rise of Alibaba 129
    Alibaba 130
    NFL Footballs "Sold Out" 132
    Why E-commerce? 135

Chapter 16 Supply Chains to Satisfy China's Super
    Consumers 139
    Supply Chain Megaprocesses 140
    Plan 141
    Buy 142
    Make 142
    Distribute 143
    Sell 144
    Aligning Strategy, Structure, and Implementation 144

Chapter 17 Segmentation 147
    Surveying China 147
    A Most Discerning Consumer 152

Chapter 18 Marketing 155
    Consumer Impulses and Desires 156
    Lenovo's Approach: The Best of Both Worlds 157
    From East to West to Wei East 161
    Baby Boom 164
    Brand Advertising in China 169
    Going Native—Tory Burch, Gossip Girl,
       and Made-for-China TV 170
    The Role of Social Media in Marketing: United States
       versus China 173
    Promotions 177

Chapter 19 The Chinese Luxury and Premium Market 179
 The Nouveau Riche: Pebble Beach or Nothing 180
 The Gifting Group 181
 China's Engine: The New Middle Class Seeks Quality
  and Value 182
 Affordable Luxury: A Tiffany's Tie Clip and an
  Entry-Level BMW 183
 China's Luxury Downturn: Myths and Realities 186

Chapter 20 Travel and Tourism 191
 Take a Walk on Boardwalk—Pass Go, Collect $200
  (Thousand!) 195

Chapter 21 Chinese Super Consumers Changing the World 203
 The Microsoft Miracle 203
 A Final Word about China's Super Consumers 207

Index 213

PREFACE

January 15, 2008

It started as another normal workday: up early for calls with China, meetings with clients, and working on a market-entry strategy for a fashion company. And then a small email with *huge* implications came in. It was an email that left us with our mouths hanging open. Steve Jobs, CEO of Apple computer, had written, asking for advice about dealing with China Mobile and launching the iPhone in China.

At the time China had about 600 million mobile handsets in use and China Mobile had nearly three quarters of the market. Steve felt that the Chinese market was integral to the company's continued growth. He was right. There are now 900 million mobile units in use in China, and in the next two years that number will reach 1.2 billion. Jobs explained to us that his negotiations with China Mobile, the largest mobile provider in China—and the world—were proceeding slowly and progress in the short term seemed unlikely.

The email was all the more surprising because it came on the day Apple launched the world's thinnest laptop, the MacBook Air, at Macworld. Steve Jobs was thinking about China on a major product-launch day.

We suggested to Steve that while it was true that China Mobile was the biggest player in China, its current technology, management, and leadership position meant that it might still be years before a deal could be struck. We suggested pursing China Unicom, a big player by any global standard, but a much smaller rival to China Mobile. The technology needed for iPhones was already in place, and they might be hungry to beat their big rival to market with the iPhone. Most importantly, a deal with China Unicom would give Apple faster access to China's consumers and time to build its brand, reputation, and market share as it explored further plans for expansion. China was growing and changing too fast to wait, we advised.

On August 28, 2009, the iPhone—through China Unicom—was launched.

Fast forward to January 16, 2014. After years of negotiations, alignment of interests, and technological developments, Apple CEO Tim Cook and China Mobile Chairman Xi Guoha took the stage at Apple's flagship store in Beijing to announce a partnership between the two technology giants. First-day preorders topped 1 million and first-year sales were estimated to be 24 million units.

While Apple still has some catching up to do to gain on market leaders Samsung, Lenovo, HTC, and others, it is on solid footing in the world's largest, fastest-growing, and most important mobile market. Because of its understanding that China's consumers were changing its industry, its business, and the world, Apple entered the market with the best short-term partner while being patient and finding the right deal with the best long-term partner. Apple has gone on to make billions of dollars by growing with and engaging China's Super Consumers.

ACKNOWLEDGMENTS

I would like to thank: our editors at Wiley, Shannon Vargo, Elizabeth Gildea, and Deborah Schindlar, for believing in us and giving us the chance to tell this timely and important story. Josh Berkman, whose developmental editing and organizational brilliance gave this book shape and form. Janet Carmosky for her mentorship and encyclopedic knowledge of all things China. Richard Berman, of Verb Factory, an outstanding writer and communications pro, for freely giving of himself and his expertise. Jim Tompkins and my colleagues at Tompkins International for believing in and supporting me. Steve Ganster, Steve Crandall, and the staff at Technomic Asia. Everyone at the Confucius Institute for Business at SUNY in New York. The good people at The China Institute. My fellow Board members and everyone at the Asian Financial Society. All of the great writers and authors whose coverage and interpretation of China over the last 15 years provided me with an education on China and big shoulders to stand on, including but certainly not limited to: Jim Fallows, Yu Hua, Peter Hessler, Evan Osnos, Gady Epstein, Adam Minter, Helen Wang, Louisa Lim, Paul French, Simon Winchester, Orville Schell, Matt Schiavenza, James McGregor, Laurie Burkitt, David Barbosa, Tim Clissold, and many others. To the men and women who have supported my career and shaped my education in Chinese business, culture, history, language, and mind-set: Winston Ma, I. Peter Wolfe, Bob Shapiro, Dan Harris, Esmond Queck, Ivy Liu, Jessie Hu, Shao Heng, Dayong Liu, Hank Sheller, Richard Guo, Wei Wang, John Yang, Suresh Dalai, Professor Lawrence Delson, Rebecca Fanin, Professor Andy Molinsky, Brian Glucroft, Dai Wenhong, and too many others to name here. Thanks to all of my clients, past and present, who have let me be a part of their China dreams. And to all my friends, family, and supporters through thick and thin: Donna, Anthony, Nicolas, and Marc Zarriello, Kevin James, Mike Del Tufo, Matt Polidoro, Brian Vanderhoof, Rob Klein, Terry Zuckerman, Adam Slavitt, Marc Maurizi, George Maurizi and Gayle Uhlenberg, Elliott Warren, Stephen Hochman, Keith Stillings, Ethan Garr, Sam Blumenfeld, the Allens, the Roodenrys family, the Biedermans, Hiten Manseta, Jay Isherwood, TTYC, the Melrose Drive crew, my classmates and teachers at Livingston High School and Seton Hall University, and most importantly I want to thank the thousands of Chinese citizens, business people, academics, and political leaders I have had the honor of meeting, working with, learning from, and befriending over the years. The kindness, openness, and generosity I have always been freely given in China has provided me with not only a great career, but a second home, a second brain, and a second life.

—Michael Zakkour

■   ■   ■

First, I want to thank my mentor Charles B. Wang, whom I met 26 years ago after nine months of cold-calling him. His faith in me and his inspiration have powered my journey as an entrepreneur, then and now.

Second, I want to thank Dunkin Donuts for giving me my first job, making donuts on the graveyard shift, so that I could pay for my college tuition and living expenses. That experience strengthened me and made me appreciate what America has to offer.

Third, I want to thank the former Brooklyn Queens Cable TV (today TimeWarner Cable) for giving me my first door-to-door sales job, which allowed me to develop and sharpen my selling skills by knocking on 165 doors every night so that I could save enough money to start my first business in 1992 and put a down payment on my first house on Long Island.

My list of gratitude is probably longer than the Yangtze River, as over the years numerous people helped me along the way and I will try to name some of them who deserve special note. First, to Jessica Juping Tu, for all her TLC and faith in me over the years. Second, to Olivia, for taking great care of Kristi and who instilled in her wonderful values and took care of her care so that I could focus on my business. Also to my current and former business partners, Thomas W. Shinick, Walter Lin, and

Albert Chin, for sticking with me throughout those years. Many business advisors and friends have also been invaluable in providing me ideas and support. Herb and Nancy Siegel, you both are my extended family and taught me about the value of a great family and friendship. Jeremiah Schnee and Margaret Poswistilo, for being my biggest supporters and strategic partners in many of my business endeavors. Stuart and Harriet Levine, who really helped me understand what writing and marketing a book really meant.

I also want to thank my Jewish uncle, Steven Dreyfus, who has been unrelenting in providing me sage advice and guidance for the last 20+ years. My Asian American entrepreneurial friends have been unwavering in giving me all kinds of support and encouragement and I want to thank them. Anil Kapoor of SVAM International, Aziz Ahmad of UTC Associates, Brian Li of A&Z Pharmaceuticals, Russell Sarder at Netcom Learning, Fred Teng, Joyce Moy, Susan Kim, Robert Wong, Tong Li, Helen Liu, Alex Peng, Rocky Zhang, Albert and Ben Wei, Lily Hui, Grace McDermott, Varghese Chacko, Naheed Syed, and all my other friends at USPAACC, to name just a few.

Other business advisors and friends that deserve my deep gratitude include Paul Schulman, Peter Cuneo and family, Dirk Junge of Pitcarin, Ron Greenstone, Peter Goldsmith, Glynis Long, Howard Cohen, Jeff Knoll, Arthur Dong, my lovely sister Wei Brian, and Will Fang and all my friends at the Cheung Kong Graduate Business School (CKGSB), Bob Quintana, Robert Reiss of the CEO Show, Greg Furman of the Luxury Marketing Council, Ira Neimark, Michael Wolff, Harvey Feinberg, and Michael Jemal. Melanie Rudin and Richard Gellman of Tourneau have been wonderful partners for my book and I want to thank them as well. Also I want to thank Sean Combs, Catherine Lin, and Ashli Sower at Ni Hao Media for their support and friendship.

Last but not least, I want to thank our editors Shannon Vargo, Elizabeth Gildea, and Elana Schulman at John Wiley & Sons, Inc., for their excellence and dedication in shepherding this book to fruition.

—Savio Chan

Introduction

The China Dream

The Chinese dream is based in historical reality, but also in the future. It is national, ethnic, and it belongs to every Chinese person. It is ours, and most of all it belongs to the young generations.

—Xi Jinping

China's leaders have traditionally used big-idea slogans to promote the ideals and governing philosophy they want to foster for the present and future of the country. These slogans, due in part to their simplicity and vagueness, pack a lot into a few words and people who know China—or want to learn about the world's most populous nation—must think deeply about them.

When they make pronouncements in slogan form, the leaders of China's central government aren't just articulating a philosophy or trying to inspire people: they are defining the vision and end point for mechanisms of legal and social development, for enterprise, and for resource management. A landmark statement by the chairman of the Communist Party is not an attempt to create a mood or inspire the population. It's a national strategy.

Deng Xiaoping, China's de facto leader from 1978 to 1992, set the stage for the early post-Mao years with his policy of "Four Modernizations" (agriculture, industry, science and technology, and the military). Deng affixed two names to the next era: *Reform and Opening* and *Socialism with Chinese Characteristics*. It was a movement that birthed the Chinese economic miracle of the past 30 years.

What he meant by socialism with Chinese characteristics was that China would pursue a path of reforms focused on market development. The deeper, unsaid, but readily understood meaning behind it was that China would abandon the ideological purity and the cult of Mao— dictatorship of the masses—in favor of something far more pragmatic: a version of the use of capital and markets that was compatible with China's own economic history, and with some non-Chinese versions of capitalism dominant in our age.

In 1992, when it seemed that power struggles within the party to reverse market reforms were gaining ground, Deng made another pro- nouncement: "To get rich is glorious." What he signaled with that bold statement was that China should work to elevate its status as a wealthy, strong nation; that individuals would be permitted to accrue private property and wealth; that ideology was taking a back seat to pragma- tism; and that pragmatism meant commitment to economic expansion backed by market-directed capital. It wasn't just an empty slogan; it was a major policy direction.

Deng's successors Jiang Zemin and Zhu Rongji were successful in implementing extensive reforms that opened numerous sectors to for- eign investment and took China into the World Trade Organization (WTO).

As the structure and direction of China's economy deviated further and further from the doctrines of communism, the new party secre- tary of China, Jiang Zemin, felt the need to develop his own vision of leadership: the *Three Represents*. Announced in 2000, the vision aimed to reconcile the direction of China's development—more social reform and more capitalist constructs—with China's political status under the Communist Party.

In other words, it was an attempt to answer an obvious question: How is it that a country led by the Communist Party is encouraging the ownership of production by private interests and the accrual of personal wealth? Jiang's Three Represents state that the party stands for:

1. The development trends of advanced productive forces.
2. The orientations of an advanced culture.
3. The fundamental interests of the overwhelming majority of China's people. (So much for collective ownership of the means of production.)

The next generation of leadership—every 10 years the composition of the standing committee of the Politburo and the two heads of party and state are reassigned—placed Hu Jintao as head of the party from 2003 to 2013. Hu governed from the foundation of two new and very powerful slogans: "Harmonious Society" and "Scientific Development." In their simplest interpretations, these meant that Chinese stability (social, government, and economic) was paramount, the government's role was to ensure that all Chinese would benefit from reforms, and that economic structures that had been proven in previous years to raise standards of living and global influence would continue. That is, while Harmonious Society makes reference to wealth inequality, it also signals a lack of intent to do anything sudden.

Xi Jinping succeeded Hu in the top post in 2013. Debuting in November 2012, Xi's new slogan, big idea, and guiding principle is "the Chinese Dream." Xi was inspired to use the slogan by the thoughts of Liu Mingfu, a retired Chinese PLA colonel, who wrote a book called *The China Dream: Great Power Thinking and Strategic Posture in the Post-America Era* in 2010. It's an obvious and likely intentional riff on the American Dream, which includes growing wealth and consumerism as well as a healthy dose of nationalism, patriotism, and military expansion. All are hallmarks of the American Dream and the first wave of American super consumers. What lies beyond the surface similarities? It is Xi's regime, and the Standing Committee in which he is the key leader, that will run China until 2023. Because cryptic pronouncements made by a top leader have a real impact on policies, it's worth looking for clues about Xi's intent. We find some in the twelfth Five-Year Plan (FYP), released in 2010.

China's political cycle ensures continuity and momentum by overlapping the terms of office with the term of the previous regime's Five-Year Plan. Xi's regime will release its own FYP in 2015, but first the government needs to complete implementation of the FYP released in 2010. Here's what the twelfth Five-Year Plan contains: a recognition that manufacturing for export—what made China the world's second-largest economy over the past 25 years—will not sustain China's growth and prosperity for the next 25 years. The reforms of the previous regimes freed hundreds of millions of Chinese from the grip of poverty, allowed numerous centers of economic activity to emerge, empowered a new super-wealthy elite, and—here's the point that sociologists, economists, political theorists, and business people worldwide now have to address—*created the largest middle class the world has ever seen while at the same time history's second group of super consumers was born*. When the twelfth FYP was being developed, China's consumption economy was exploding and it has since grown exponentially.

And the twelfth Five-Year Plan makes it clear that China's leadership wants the consumption economy to grow more. There isn't enough margin or productivity in low-value exports to support rising standards of living across the parts of Chinese society that are still poor. The twelfth FYP is designed to push the Chinese people to loosen their wallets further, to spend more, and to spend on more services. It addresses management of forestry, water, and land resources; aerospace and military; hospital and educational systems; countless aspects of economic and social development that two- or four-year-term legislators in multiparty systems could not imagine dealing with as a national-policy exercise. It also names sectors for further liberalization, including a few high-margin, capital-intensive, very-large-scale services sectors—such as finance, insurance, and real estate—sectors that sell, in effect, a sense of security and stability.

Thus, we know Xi means that the Chinese Dream is based in a stable state as well as a healthy and higher-productivity economy with more consumption and more services. Basically, this means people pursuing a good living and being encouraged to spend freely.

But did the average Chinese citizen see the Chinese Dream in the same way?

In 2003, I (Michael) had a long lunch with an intern from my Beijing office. We talked at length about her upbringing, her role in our company, and her ongoing education. She was a student at Fudan University in Shanghai, one of the most prestigious in China (China's Yale to Tsinghua University's Harvard).

I asked her what she hoped for after graduation. She answered with one word: *Freedom*. I had been in China long enough at that point to realize that that was a loaded word and an even more loaded subject, one that might not be appropriate to dig too deeply into over a casual lunch with a young person working in my office.

Nonetheless, I asked her what she meant. Her answer surprised me then; it makes more sense to me now.

She said, "I want to be free to find a great job, a great career, to make a lot of money, and to spend it as I see fit."

I was taken aback by her answer. It might have been my China naiveté, my American sense of what "freedom" meant, or the inherent taking for granted that I was born into a country and culture where that desire was a given. But that was the moment I realized that my career would shift; that the future for me would be not only be in production and supply chains but in helping companies, their products, brands, and services in China. The white light moment was seeing the melding of the three most important business stories of the last thirty years—The Rise of China as Producer and Consumer, The Internet and E-Commerce Boom, The Growth of Modern Global Supply Chains—come together. My focus from 2005 onwards has been on helping companies leverage these three phenomena. Tompkins Asia, where I work, has provided the perfect platform to do exactly that. U.S. China Partners, the consulting firm that Savio runs, went through a similar process. Initially focused on production, for the past 10 years Savio has worked with Western businesses by fostering partnerships in China that help their products and brands succeed in China.

That lunch was my epiphany. I saw that someday China would be the largest and perhaps most important consumer market in the world. In 2003 that view was not all that common. Aside from a few luxury brands and the largest, most fast-moving consumer goods (FMCG)–focused *Fortune* 500 companies, not many brands were focused on selling to the consumer market in China.

Ten years later, as Xi introduced the Chinese Dream, Savio and I talked about that lunch. Here was China's development in a nutshell: a smart and ambitious young woman, graduating at a time when she had opportunities to make a great living—not only to support herself and her family, but to buy the things she *wanted*, not just what she *needed*.

She personified the shift from poor to middle income, from manufacturing for a living wage to consumption based on a high salary. To her, freedom was about education, employment, financial stability, and becoming a consumer. We could quote hundreds of Chinese citizens in every type of media round the world who said and say things very similar to our intern, and there are millions in China who feel this way as proven out by our research and that of others.

In the years since that lunch, China has fulfilled that intern's dream, and those of millions of others just like her. In the coming years, hundreds—yes, hundreds—of millions more Chinese will have their dreams of material prosperity and a stable life fulfilled, too. Today, they are the current and future members of China's super consumer mega-class, their sophistication and spending power growing at a rate that reminds us of the original super consumers: the American baby boomers.

So, how much do the American Dream and the Chinese Dream have in common?

The similarities include a sense of patriotism and cultural confidence, a backdrop of emergence from the dark period of their parents' generation (the Great Depression and WWII vs. the decades of ideological struggle and poverty before and under Mao), new national and personal wealth, a developing highway system and car culture, a desire for the better things in life, and emerging hyper-consumerism.

Yet there are very significant differences: For starters, the demographics and diversity of early twenty-first century China are nothing like those of 1950s America. Then there are the deep structural issues: the legacy of economic models whose roots extend back thousands of years; a philosophical landscape based in the long-term influences of Confucianism, Taoism, and Buddhism (mixed in with some recent Maoism); and some obviously (and profound yet not-so-obviously) different conceptions of politics, society, and sense of the self.

We feel it's fair to say that the American Dream and the Chinese Dream, not to mention the distinct modern European Dream, have enough in common that we should use our knowledge of those dreams when making sense of the economic trends in China now, yet account for the Chinese-ness of the Chinese Dream. What is the most obvious commonality? On the surface it is the desire to have a career, to own a business, to get rich, to own a house and a car, to raise a family, and to have a long and healthy life that includes a great deal of material, cultural, and political comfort and security.

That said, we need to be careful of any ideas that may imply the commercial infrastructure or the specifics of consumer psychology are fundamentally similar to the United States or Europe. There is a unique roadmap for selling to Chinese consumers—to help them live the dream—and while the destination may look the same, the journey is necessarily quite different.

Our Intent

This is not a book about how to do business in China nor is it a book that promises "10 Rules," "5 Keys," "The Secret," "A Comprehensive Guide to … Branding, Partnerships, E-Commerce, etc.," in China. Nor is it an academic history of consumerism in China. Rather, this is an exploration of a new phenomenon, China's super consumers, as explained through history, culture, language, and mind-set and most importantly by those engaging with them. It's a look at what motivates them; what, where, when, and how they buy; and what it means for you, your company, and the world—today and in the next 10 years.

In this book, we will explore how the first 2,000 years of China's history set the stage for the emergence of a super-consumer class, and how China's history shapes the psychology of consumers and the businesses that sell to them. We will explain why foreign countries and companies have had difficulty trying, in previous eras and now, to break into the market and sell to China's consumers—whether they are a mass market of one billion or a more-defined group of 400 million, 500 million, or 700 million. We will look at how and why a Chinese consumer class was born 30 years ago and how its members became super consumers who are changing the world.

We will also share the experiences and insights of a selection of companies and executives, who we feel represent many others, who have succeeded in engaging with and selling to Chinese super consumers.

We hope you will learn from and identify with these stories to either improve or begin your engagement with China's super consumers. It is our purpose to explain who China's super consumers are, who is selling to them, what and why they are buying, and how they are changing the world by telling the stories of the executives, brands, and retailers worldwide who are succeeding. It is our opinion and experience that China is too vast, too diverse, and too contradictory, and changes too fast for there to be hard and fast rules or a secret sauce. Our intent rather is to provide you with a solid foundation, based on history, and facts to help you better understand what you can do to ensure you are part of this business/social/consumer revolution, and not a victim of it.

The Country within a Country

To get a sense of the scale of the world inhabited by the Chinese super consumer, consider this for a moment: China has a population, depending on who you talk to and what statistics you use, between 1.2 and 1.5 billion people. The United States is the third most populous country on Earth at about 320 million people, and is the largest consumer society on Earth (for now), and yet as a market, the United States is China's rounding error. Similarly, Europe's population is more than 400 million people, and China is likely to have almost 500 million online shoppers by 2015.

China's current consumer revolution, at least for now, is largely powered by the 400 million or so inhabitants of *the country within the country*: coastal China. Not all of this region is actually on the water—Beijing is dry as a desert—but all of the provinces and cities to which the term refers are close enough to the coast (and the trade activities with the West) to have benefited directly from Reform and Opening. "Coastal China" includes the Bohai Bay cities of Dalian, Qingdao, Tianjin, and Beijing; Shanghai and its two neighboring provinces of Jiangsu (Nanjing, Wuxi, Suzhou) and Zhejiang (Hangzhou, Ningbo, Wenzhou); across the straits from Taiwan is Fujian province (Fuzhou, Xiamen); and the megacities of the Pearl River Delta (Guangzhou, Shenzhen, Dongguan, Huizhou, and Hong Kong).

The fact that the majority of super consumers reside in the country-within-the-country holds great promise and potentially great peril for China as well as for the companies whose future, in some way, relies on continued growth in the Middle Kingdom.

The upshot is that further inland there are 500 to 700 million more consumers who, due to a number of economic and social factors, have yet to transition from low or midlevel consumers to super consumers. The downside is that if China does not develop new consumer regions and classes rapidly, ensure income distribution across China, and create social and political realities on the ground that will provide more disposable income, then China's growth could be hindered and its potential as the world's top consumer market could be threatened.

Before we dive into the background and the backdrop of the past—the culture and history that shape China's super consumers—let's consider a few more facts to add to the population/consumer scale facts we mentioned above.

- GM sold more than 3 million cars in China in 2013 and expects to sell 5 million or more in 2015 and 2016. China is Audi's most important market, and Porsche expects China to be its biggest market within a year.

- Thirsty Chinese consume more beer and wine by volume than any country on Earth.
- Chanel, Louis Vuitton, and Prada are the three most desired luxury brands in China, and each derives a significant percentage of their profits from China sales.
- Coach's second-largest market is in China (in fiscal 2013, Coach's sales on China's mainland, Hong Kong, Macao, and Taiwan reached $430 million, a 40 percent year-on-year increase), and China has made Michael Kors the most searched for brand on the Internet.
- All of the 2013 top 10 power brands in China were foreign.
- Only caffeine freaks in the United States drink more Starbucks coffee than those in China (China recently passed Canada as the company's number-two market).
- Hershey predicts China will be its second-largest market within five years.
- China is the world's largest market for musical instruments.
- Gucci has *three times* as many stores in Beijing as it does in New York, and Louis Vuitton's new Shanghai store has the floor space to rival its Champs-Élysées flagship.
- China also has an estimated 700 billionaires and more than a million and a half millionaires (putting it in third place after Japan and the United States).
- McKinsey & Co. has forecast that by 2015 upper-middle-class Chinese consumers with annual incomes from $15,000 to $30,000 will account for almost one-quarter of the nation's luxury-good purchases.
- Of all the emerging markets named in the 2000s as the BRICS (Brazil, Russia, India, China, and South Africa), only China has maintained rapid growth and expansion.

It is not hard to see why companies from around the world look to Chinese consumers—young and old, male and female, from Beijing or Qingdao, online or off, wearing the brightly colored costumes of superheroes—to swoop in and rescue them from static and even dying markets in the United States and Europe.

They are changing the world—so much so, that purchase decisions made in Shanghai now have ripple effects on the lives and livelihoods of people from Lagos to Los Angeles. They are changing the way companies design, build, market, and sell their products. They are changing the balance of trade on a global scale. They are making and breaking brands. They are changing the way bricks-and-mortar and e-commerce retail takes place *everywhere*, not just in China. Their shopping habits and attitudes, channel preferences, and communication patterns are changing the very idea of what it means to plan, make, buy, move, store, and sell products around the world.

They are changing businesses in obvious and hidden ways. In short, China's super consumers are changing China and the world in ways unimaginable even 10 years ago. The questions for you are: Are you a beneficiary or victim of this phenomenon, and what are you doing about it?

PART I

History, Culture, and Language Matter—The Birth of Chinese Consumerism

CHAPTER 1

From Feudalism
to Fendi

China is often talked about and understood in the media, in board-rooms, at consultancies (present company included), and at design houses through the use of mind-blowing statistics, superlatives, and clichés. Some of them are true, some embellished, some misunderstood, and some are just misleading.

Getting past the hype, hyperbole, and superlatives, we need to ask and answer some real questions. When did China start to consume en masse? Who's winning? Who's losing? What role do foreign companies have in the boom? What role do domestic Chinese companies play? What can the world learn from China? What can China learn from the world? Is it a zero-sum game? What do we really know and under-stand about super consumerism in China? Where are its cultural and historic roots? What patterns of China's long economic history are being repeated or amplified? What patterns are brand new?

Also, when did Westerners first realize the potential importance of Chinese consumers? When did they start dreaming of selling their best wares to the largest population on Earth? Prior to the past 30 years, did any of them crack the market and succeed?

Let's start with two incontrovertible facts. First, China is really big and really old. As such, the nation's sense of itself is both intense and deeply embedded. Western firms that overfocus on the country's twentieth century political history—that see the behaviors of Chinese people as a response to or backlash against communism—are missing the bigger picture. China has been a major world power and an economic superpower several times in its long history. Second, it needs to be said—and let it be said here with no ambiguity—China isn't a Johnny-come-lately on the world scene, suffering from a lack of sophistication and ready to embrace whatever the West brings. China knows itself and will embrace what is consistent with its self-image.

Still, at the dawn of the twentieth century, most parts of China were operating as feudal economies. Thirty years ago, after socialist construction of basic infrastructure from 1949 to 1979, there was still virtually no consumer economy. But by 2013, China was seen as the world's top market for luxury goods. So, how has China moved, in the past 100 years, from feudalism to Fendi? What happened that Chinese society gave rise to hundreds of millions—or even, as James McGregor named them in his seminal 2005 book—*One Billion Customers*?

The first part of this book will explain the history, culture, and mind-set that shaped China's super consumers. The second part will define who they are and why, where, when, and how they buy. It will also chronicle the stories of the executives, companies and brands from around the world, and China, who have succeeded in understanding and selling to China's super consumers.

Back to the Future

So, what does it look and feel like when the balance of trade, commerce, and power in the world you once knew no longer exists? What does it look and feel like when the globalized world that you just got used to—China as the world's factory, America as the wallet—turns 180 degrees?

What does it look and feel like when the Chinese Dream becomes reality and China super consumers change the world?

It *looks* like Yan Wu, a 28-year-old advertising executive from a small village on the Yellow River—now living and working in Shanghai— arriving at the Jing An Temple Starbucks at eight o'clock in the morning to buy her prework coffee. She walks to the counter in her

Michael Kors shoes. She is wearing a stylish, sheer Zara blouse (hanging loosely over her Levi's jeans) and she is carrying a Tory Burch handbag.

She takes a 100 RMB note from her Fendi wallet, pays about 33 RMB (more than $6) for her latte, and sits down at an empty table. She applies some eyeliner that she bought at the Sephora flagship store at Nanjing West Road over the weekend, washes down some GNC vitamins (bought at the new Shanghai GNC at Raffles City), and spends the next 15 minutes checking email, texting on WeChat, and buying a new skirt on Tao Bao—all done on her domestically made HTC phone.

It looks and feels like a force of nature, a once-in-a-century tsunami of change that is rippling across the ocean, crashing onto shore, and rolling into the executive suites and boardrooms of companies of all shapes and sizes, from all over the globe, and rolling back out again to wash away the world as we know it.

It looks and feels very much like the era of Globalization 1.0 (roughly 1978 to 2008) is over. In fact, it feels like what is happening must be Globalization 2.0, where China's importance is not as a manufacturing center, or even as consumer market, but as a place that sets the standards for speed and effectiveness in distribution, retail, digital and mobile marketing, branding, and design. It feels like an era where companies from around the world have to rethink and reset their strategies according to who and where their newest and most important customers are, where to make goods, and how to deliver them on a global basis, because the 1.0 models don't apply anymore.

If it looks and feels like the perfect storm of rising wealth, urbanism, globalism, and hyperconsumerism, all helped along by favorable government policies, that's probably because it is.

Ms. Yan and hundreds of millions of people like her are today's super consumers, drawing the world's investments, people, brands, and focus to the shores of the Middle Kingdom. Consider what changes came to the world's manufacturers and marketers the last time a class of super consumers emerged. The baby boomers of America changed the twentieth century; what they wanted and bought, the rest of the world wanted and bought. The brands they liked expanded worldwide, spread American soft power globally, and helped usher in what came to be called the American Century. Are we now living at the dawn of the Chinese Century?

Chinese Consumption: What's Old Is New Again (Tenfold!)

Historically, China has been the world's economic superpower. If we wanted to create a controversy, we could find the data to argue that the past 400 years of Anglo/European dominance in science, technology, and sheer economic power as share of global GDP, are not a historical inevitability, but an anomaly from a longer-established pattern of Chinese economic dominance.

Counterintuitively, throughout most of China's history (even when it was a dominant economy and regional power) there was not a large consumer class focused on spending on wants and needs. There was the Imperial Court and the civil servants (often called mandarins) who ran national, regional, and local capitals, and a small military and commercial elite. Beyond that there was nothing we'd call a consumer class. People traded for and bought food and the essentials of work, family, and survival. There was a bimodal distribution of income—a tiny blip of elites at the high end, and a huge mass of poor, illiterate labor at the bottom.

Even in recent Chinese history, Chinese consumerism was but a dream, dreamed by both aspiring buyers and frustrated would-be sellers. In the twentieth century, from the founding of the People's Republic in 1949 until the mid-1980s—when Deng Xiaoping's early reforms allowed more trade and sale of manufactured goods—consumer culture in China did not exist.

For most of these four decades, all manufacturing, trading, and distribution was handled by state-owned enterprises (SOEs). They made and moved goods between producers and the people. The term *consumer* can't really be applied, because there was virtually no retail, no surplus income, and no choice. Nothing from outside China was legally sold and bought. In urban China, ration coupons provided grain, meat, and oil to work units to which everyone was attached, either as a worker or as a family member. Liquor, beer, and soap came in one brand—whatever was made locally. And items that were for sale were cheap. We're talking 20 cents for a bowl of noodles, 30 cents for a bowl of draft beer. Everything else—crackers, yarn, and bicycles—were sold by state-owned department stores.

Nowhere after 1920 was Henry Ford's maxim that "You can buy a Ford in any color you want, as long as it's black" truer than in China. Do you want your Mao suit in blue or gray?

Had our archetypical super consumer, Ms. Yan, been alive at any time between 1949 and Deng's first reforms, she'd have been assigned to a work unit at a state-run company, living in housing administered by her work unit—with others from that work unit—and eating her daytime and perhaps evening meals with her colleagues at the unit cafeteria. These would not have been choices but rather the sole manner for economic and social viability.

Her wardrobe would have consisted of five or six simple jackets, hats, and pants—in gray, green, or navy—hand-knit sweaters, cloth shoes, no makeup, uncomfortable undergarments, and a canvas bag. Her only drink would have been tea; TCM (traditional Chinese medicines) would have been her vitamins. Even if makeup had been available, she would not risk seeming bourgeois, anti-revolutionary, or spiritually polluted by wearing it. With no legal imports of consumer goods and no private enterprise, a factory organized on the principle of utilitarian production for the Chinese people would make up every material object she encountered.

The idea of an economy based on the consumption of goods and services, not production—the idea of dreams of comfort and not utility—was unthinkable. The socially confining effects of three decades under Mao would fade gradually through the 1980s and early 1990s.

Considering that private telephones of almost any kind were nonexistent until the late 1980s and private ownership of a car only became possible in the mid-1990s, considering that the streets of Beijing, Shanghai, and most Chinese cities are thronging with people driving cars and using smartphones, considering that Shenzhen did not exist as an actual city in 1985, and that there were donkey carts on the streets of PuDong in Shanghai until the mid-1990s, we ought to ask ourselves what happened that made such a fast transformation possible? What is the commercial infrastructure that made it happen? What is the psychology of the hundreds of millions of people, like Ms. Yan, who have experienced a rocket trip from poverty to posh, from feudalism to Fendi?

The timeline, roughly, proceeds as follows. About a decade and a half after the fall of Mao, China had a nascent retail sector, some taxicabs, some privately owned small restaurants and clothing shops, and numerous other ways to consume that essentially had not existed for 40 years.

In addition to some early foreign-style shopping experiences, the development of private industry and market-based employment was exploding in the 1990s. Large numbers of Chinese began to find themselves with disposable income, and they were looking for places to spend it. Beijing was the earliest location for foreign engagement, so it had the earliest foreign-invested retail outlets: the Lufthansa Center, the Lido shopping center, and the Saite. These were where foreign-made cosmetics and electric razors, imported suits, and toasters could be acquired. Small businesses were opening, private corporations were forming and operating, and foreign investment was flowing in. Non-Chinese food became available outside of hotels. Hong Kong–invested Maxim's opened some locations in Guangzhou. In Beijing, the Baskin-Robbins ice cream store, operating in the state-owned Friendship Store, was the earliest foreign-branded restaurant.

By 1994, China's first foreign-invested shopping centers were under construction in Shanghai as well as Beijing. In apparel, Nike and the Hong Kong brand Giordano, Canadian-in-exile garment brand Ports, and Italy's Ermenegildo Zegna were among the retail pioneers to open single-brand, stand-alone storefronts. They did so working with determination and creativity—based on their massive investment in local expertise—within the strictures of a regulatory regime that very clearly prohibited foreign participation in retail and distribution.

In 1999, when the first Starbucks opened in China, the cities of Shanghai, Beijing, and Shenzhen each had about five large shopping centers filled with counters selling merchandise made by foreign and domestic companies—almost always private rather than state-owned producers. Carrefour had figured out how to open hypermarkets that sold bread and wine, duvets, and kitchenware. The transition from feudalism to Fendi was beginning.

China's Growth Is Different

While China is not the world's only developing country with a fast growing, increasingly wealthy population that is making more and spending more, it is by far the largest and most important.

From about 2002 until 2010, millions of words were written in newspapers, magazines, and books about the dual rise of the Indian and Chinese economies and the important role the consumers of both countries would play in shaping their domestic and world economies. It wasn't long ago that Tiger-versus-Dragon cover stories were a regular occurrence, and business conferences were organized around BRIC or emerging-market clusters: Brazil, Russia, Indonesia, Vietnam, and South Africa. There has long been conversation among economists and trend watchers as to which countries should be watched as major movers in global growth, development, trade, and consumer culture.

But, as the dust has settled, only China has kept growth at extraordinarily high levels, and only China has produced a new breed of super consumer.

We asked Janet Carmosky, a lifelong China hand whose passion is explaining the relevance of history and culture to commerce, why. Why China? She says, "China's prosperity is a direct result of the power, the depth and energy, the fluidity, the resilience, the inclusiveness, and the intelligence of the Chinese culture. The collective memory of this culture tells them to hunker down when necessary—for as long as necessary—and to make hay while the sun shines. Right now, the sun is shining."

About the pace of change in the business landscape and the habits of consumers, Carmosky says, "China has enormously deep cultural roots, like the tap roots of trees that can survive in the most arid of climates. These roots both define the nation's essential identity, as it has evolved over millennia, and allow for very quick adaptation. As long as the change is compatible with cultural identity and values, it can take place virtually overnight, and on a massive scale."

China business years can be like dog years: Fifty-two weeks can transform the business and consumer landscape in ways that would take half a decade in the United States or Europe.

From our perspective as business consultants in China, it boils down to fewer words: Your China strategy has a six-month shelf life; after that, it stinks.

Therefore, some key lessons regarding the market are:

- History, mind-set, and culture should be your guide.
- Nonstop innovation and change are a must.
- Your brand/product/service/company story matters but must be contextualized for China.

While we hope you find all of the information, history, stories, facts, and figures in this book to be interesting and useful, we have especially high hopes that the stories of the brands, companies, and executives who found, and in many cases created, the formula for successful branding, distribution, and selling to China's super consumers will be of particular use. There is no better way to understand the Chinese consumers and engage them than by listening to and learning from those who have done it—both Chinese and foreign.

CHAPTER 2

Orientation

A nation's culture resides in the hearts and in the soul of its people.
—Gandhi

When we advise companies on entering, growing, or changing course in China, we always start with a deep background on culture and history.

"Why?" some of our clients ask. "We didn't come to you for a history lesson or a course in Chinese sociology and ethnology. We came to you for strategy to operate and sell in China" or "I can take language lessons on Rosetta Stone; I don't think any of this language or history stuff is relevant."

It is. Knowing *their* history and culture is a prerequisite for understanding and succeeding with Chinese consumers.

You don't personally have to master the Chinese language, culture, history, and mindset to be successful in China. But you have to listen to the people who have done so. Otherwise, one can too easily see the suits and the coffee, the wine, and the BMWs, and conclude that China is a westernized society. It's too simplistic to conclude that appealing to Chinese consumers should be no different from appealing to consumers in a Western culture, say, Brazil—or an Asian market that also developed since the 1970s, say Korea or Japan, and it is also too simplistic to assume they don't respond to many of the things we do; rather you want to find that right mix between change everything and change nothing for China.

Chinese culture, commercial infrastructures, and society have a deeply established logic all their own, built over long periods of time. Creating trust, fostering peer recommendations, and building personal relationships with Chinese customers is a must—and they all depend on your understanding of the culture.

Even the most sophisticated of consumer marketing giants can be tripped up by something as obvious as the importance of language. Early translations into Chinese for the quintessential brand, Coca-Cola, actually used completely inappropriate written characters to render the phonetics of the brand name. Sure, "ke kou le la" sounds right, but every syllable in Chinese has numerous homonyms. If the characters mean "bite the wax tadpole," then you've completely failed to meet the Chinese in the hallway of cultural relevance.

Fortunately when Coke reentered China after Reform and Opening it knew to put some resources into understanding the importance of language. It researched 40,000 characters to find a phonetic equivalent that also translated to something meaningful and descriptive about the product: "Ke kou ke le," 可口可乐, "Happiness in the Mouth."

Coke wasn't the only beverage company to underestimate the importance of language. When Pepsi entered China, it launched with the slogan, "Pepsi Brings You Back to Life." It found the proper Chinese translation and launched its campaign. What Pepsi didn't realize was that the phrase, due to improper translation, was "Pepsi brings your ancestors back from the grave." This is not a good marketing strategy in a country where ancestor worship is an important part of the culture.

More recently we had to advise a home-decoration company about its overreliance on white candles. In China, white candles are a sign of death and funerals.

The response we get from many business leaders is not surprising. Most international business people understand that some allowance has to be made for differences in culture, law, logistics, and tastes when entering new markets. But many do not understand the profound and myriad differences that exist between China and the United States, Germany, France, or Brazil.

When a Canadian company does business in England, an American company markets in France, or a Brazilian company in Spain, there is shared sense of history, culture, language, and attitudes about life's meaning. Yes, there are some major and many minor differences between the cultures and tastes of consumers, but they all operate from a fairly consistent cultural blueprint. Consider that Western nations share some major cultural and historical factors:

- A knowledge of and values based in Judeo-Christian religion, philosophy, and guiding principles
- A Newtonian understanding of science
- Founding principles of modern society in the Enlightenment
- A Smithian understanding of free markets
- A long history of democracy, free markets, and consumerism
- A linear understanding of time and history
- Business conducted in a transactional manner
- A European foundation of society and culture that was spread to North and South America, Oceania, and other regions
- A common alphabet
- Similar foods and drink, and a culture that celebrates with alcohol
- A philosophical orientation towards individual freedom and identity

China on the other hand has:

- A Confucian/Buddhist/Taoist religio-philosophical tradition, and a government that openly declares itself atheist
- A circular and cyclical understanding and sense of time, history, and relationships
- An almost purely Chinese foundation of societal and cultural norms, so powerful that they have shaped the societies and norms of Japan, the Koreas, and Southeast Asia over the course of 3,000 years. There was an abundance of culture exported out of China, but very little culture imported in
- The written language uses 30,000 characters—not letters—providing for much more nuance than Western languages and alphabets
- Colors and number have an outsize significance in China that is almost nonexistent in the West
- A long history of commerce, driven by government and conducted by clans
- An intense and passionate food culture (while Chinese people drink alcohol, the culture is far more centered on food than drinking)
- Status, identity, and sense of security are grounded in the group

It is important to learn what shapes Chinese society, culture, and thinking before you can sell a product or service to its consumers.

Those hoping to connect with China's super consumers must absorb and internalize the fact that success or failure will largely hinge on an understanding of the Chinese nation's self-image, its diverse regions, and its individuals. China's deep roots in history, language, philosophy, and culture trump the convergence theory, which states that once people achieve a certain threshold of disposable income, they will spend in similar patterns to people at similar disposable income levels in other cultures.

The mind-set of the Chinese businessperson and consumer creates the consumer's self-image; his idea of his place in society and the universe; and his ambitions, needs, desires, likes, and dislikes. The mind-set translates to purchase motivators. Purchase motivators will and must determine your product design, shape, size, color, price, selling channel, branding, marketing, and benefits.

Often when a company or product fails in China, it is because these cultural building blocks—history language, philosophy, and culture—were not a central focus from day one.

Just to make this even more interesting, here's a fact that might be obvious given the geography of China and the length of time over which regional differences have evolved: China and Chinese people are not monoliths. We approach China as 22 distinct markets. (More on that in later chapters.) As a start, consider that China is continental in size and is quite diverse in climate, geography, cultural influences, language, food, esthetic values, and spiritual beliefs. Now factor in China's collective memory. Over the course of 4,000 years of civilization, the Chinese have seen and been many things: sometimes powerful and sometimes weak, wealthy and poor, an occupying power, and an occupied country. The reason you need to know Chinese history is because the Chinese, consciously or not, define themselves by their history.

A Code to the Chinese Mind-set

So what makes the Chinese consumer Chinese? If we say that history and culture should be your guide, what map do we use? There are a lot of smart people who have spent long years understanding, working in, and selling to China, so there are a lot of guides and maps.

For this book, we're picking the one developed by Janet Carmosky. She's a bilingual, bicultural, self-described culture geek who has been working in US–China business since 1985. For 18 years, she was part of a Xi'an-based family of party officials and wife to an ambitious, bilingual Chinese man who prospered as one of the earliest returnees. (A Chinese-born person who gets an overseas education then returns to China to work, hopefully on the same terms as a foreign national.)

From 2003 until 2013, she lived back in the United States, trying to integrate and explain her Chinese and American traits. When she started to talk to U.S. businesspeople in America about the Chinese mind-set, they were indignant. They wanted to know, "Why don't the Chinese keep their promises? Why don't contracts get implemented? Why won't the general manager make a decision? Don't they understand win–win? Do they even care about the long term?" Rather than simply answering their questions directly, she drew from her life experiences to design a framework for the psychology behind these and other common frustrations.

Thus her eight key contrasts between the value systems of America/ the West and China/Asia, presented in Table 2.1. While these insights

Table 2.1   Eight Key Contrasts between the Value Systems of America/the West and China/Asia

Chinese/East Asian Value	American/Western Value
1. The unit of society: Group identity	Self-sufficiency
2. The domain of scarcity: Money	Time
3. The practice of heroism: Practice restraint	Take action
4. The resolution of conflict: Minimize	Surface
5. The containment of risk: Fluidity	Rigor
6. The origin of wealth: Top down	Bottom up
7. The source of security: Clan loyalty	Civil institutions
8. The existence of absolutes: Ambiguity as truth	Pressure to discern

were developed to help executives who deal with commercial, regulatory, and workplace dynamics in China, they are nevertheless true at the level of individuals and consumers.

In short, if you're tempted to see Chinese behavior as a variation of Western behavior when creating sales, marketing, and distribution strategies, check this list. Because, as Janet says, "Sure, the Chinese do in fact think exactly the same way we do, except they have different definitions of what time, money, courage, risk, security, family, job, truth, and success mean.

"Everyone who has ever spent time trying to work across the Western–China cultural barrier knows the frustration. We try to understand why processes stall or escalate; money is spent or not spent; products are bought or ignored; people are on board or resistant; information is withheld or shared; and why innocuous questions are avoided, while questions we think are tough seem like no big deal. Here's the reality: Cultures in China and the United States use hard-coded value systems that contrast in profound, fundamental ways. Tactics and gamesmanship get us through sometimes. But being able to see past the behavior to the psychology, and past the psychology to the values—accepting that the values are not going to change—is what gets us to a higher level of understanding."

Carmosky found some visuals—now very famous—by Yang Liu, a Chinese expatriate artist in Germany, who was also working with the raw material of what makes East and West so different. From Yang Liu's series, East and West Designs, she picked and shares here her understanding of three of them (Contacts, Problem Solving, and Self-Expression). It was a start to shifting American thinking away from the explanations that our Judeo-Christian, democracy-loving culture offers (for example, "Chinese people can't be trusted" or "Communism made people lazy") and towards something more productive ("How can I get them to respect me enough to share information?" "What else is going on that the schedule keeps slipping?").

The words and images are meant to provoke the realization that we act differently because we see the world differently. The Chinese mind-set is one where the distance between a problem and a solution is not by default straight, transparent, or immediate. Where people see themselves as so interconnected, all actions either carefully align with the larger context, or they are counterproductive.

Business and Culture in Chinese and Western Worlds

USA

- Transaction oriented
- Believe in the primacy of the contract
- Take the org chart at face value
- Emphasize strategy
- Act as individuals in teams
- Distinct personal and professional lives
- View work tasks as automatic
- Surface conflict

China

- Relationship oriented
- Respond to practical and present reality
- Navigate by status, prestige
- Maximize opportunity
- Survive by managing group dynamics
- Do business with people they like
- See business as a sport
- Bury conflict

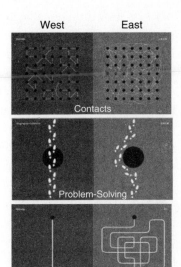

Figure 2.1 Business and Culture in Chinese and Western Worlds

Source: Janet Carmosky 2004; Drawings by Yang Liu.

Look at the Contacts picture in Figure 2.1. It shows the difference between Chinese social networks—with numerous links, widely spread, all interconnected—and Western ones, which are limited, point-to-point relationships with those closest to us. In workplace terms, the Chinese model of contacts means that group dynamics are fluid; that Chinese people field and process more information from numerous sources; and that complex and interconnected relationships—including business ones—are the norm.

Basically, the Chinese are intensely social creatures, always tallying the strength and state of their networks and extremely conscious of their place in the hierarchy. This has a direct effect on what Chinese consumers buy, where they travel, what real estate they invest in, and which brands they love.

In any culture, our networks are where we find security and gain and display prestige. Look at the pictures in the West column.

In America, if our spouse and boss are happy with us, and we take a vacation every year with the same couple, most of us feel stable and satisfied. We grab a beer or coffee with a friend once in a while. In China, people go to dinner in groups of 6 to 10. Busy Chinese at high-income brackets eat dinners and lunches out most days of the week, with many different groups. Networks cut across socioeconomic brackets—including childhood friends, school friends, relatives, and extended networks of hometown. Not everyone has gotten rich in postreform China, and those who have done better share their good fortune among their networks in many ways, gift giving among them. Networks are the single most important source of money, security, and status in China. When a friend comes to town on an unexpected visit, chances are that everyone will find time to be with her, feed her, and put her up.

Compare that with life in the United States, where old friends and even family members, when they hear you are in town for a few days, can't possibly get away. "Bobby has a Little League game," or "I just put a chicken in the oven." "Too bad! Hey, some other time." Nuclear family is the core of American life, but history has taught the Chinese to have the biggest, strongest safety nets they can manage. That is the web of contacts that you see in the pictures representing the East.

It takes a huge amount of energy to maintain a big network. Sometimes it is exhausting. But networks are crucial to survival, so the Chinese make them a priority. The giving and receiving of gifts, along with the sharing of food, are the daily practices in network maintenance. Likewise, preserving an image of success and abundance is a net contribution to the overall sense of well-being in the network, as well as the individual. Thus badge brands and face-giving experiences with documentation of such are critical.

The second picture in Figure 2.1, Problem Solving, belongs in a slide deck about working with the Chinese. It has some implications for selling to the Chinese as well. "The customer is always right" doesn't begin to describe the importance of gentleness in resolving issues. If the customer broke the watch and now wants to return it, a Chinese manager should handle that conversation.

In broader terms, the Chinese have a way of putting things behind them, without dealing directly. Part of the role that China's collective memory serves is to raise the skeletons of the past at some future moment when it isn't quite so scary to deal with them.

The Self-Expression picture in Figure 2.1 shows the 10,000-word story that everyone who works between China and the United States knows. Americans talk. We think about something, we feel something, we tell someone. Politicians, teachers, parents, and psychologists develop sophisticated processes to decide whether or not to speak about something, to whom, and how and when to say it. But in most cases, for most people, our natural tendency is to just put it right out there: "I don't like her." We confront: "You said something that hurt my feelings." We confess: "I think I just did something wrong." In a Chinese context, where people are all connected, where history has told us that bad things happen to good people, coming right out and saying what you think is risky.

Disclosure is a process of feeling out the kindest and safest way to bring out bad news. Persuasion is a walk around the garden, not a presentation of compelling facts. That's the path of many turns that Yang Liu's picture shows.

The very structure of our two languages—English and Mandarin—shapes our expressive styles. English serves as the language of international business, treaties, and law in large part because it is precise. With a very large number of words, verb tenses, cases, articles, and sentence structures, English forces us to be either clear or grammatically incorrect. Chinese is much the opposite. Every word has numerous homonyms. Elliptical sentences—omitting the subject—are common. Nouns do not have objective or subjective cases and singular or plural forms. There is no definite article. Verbs have no tenses. Everything about the Chinese language is contextual. Precision is not only completely optional but also nearly impossible to achieve.

How do the Chinese understand each other, then? Well, they get to know each other. They spend time together, they share history, and they learn to read each other, respect their silences, and treasure their confidences. They have to figure each other out.

In business, the takeaway is, be persistent in the pursuit of clarity. Ask a lot of questions. Follow up. Triple check. Do not assume that your colleagues have told you about every obstacle that's come up. Do not assume that everything discussed translated into an action plan. You may think you have been clear, that they have been clear. Follow up. If you're accountable for details and schedules to an American boss, you'll have to put more energy than you expect into staying on top of a team that really would rather not tell you everything that is going on.

How does the Chinese style of self-expression relate to consumers? Simply put, a spare apartment is more useful to a friend in hard times than a shoulder to cry on. Treating a friend to a meal, the use of your car and driver, a vacation, a spa trip, clothing, or jewelry expresses the esteem in which you hold him and the hopes you have for him. In America, we have support groups and long talks with our loved ones. In China, retail therapy isn't the only game in town, but its close.

While we could fill volumes on the scope, nature, and implications of Chinese history, culture, and mind-set; its current political, social and cultural norms; and its resulting consumer behavior, we will limit ourselves here to some key historical facts and events that have helped create and shape the Chinese super consumer. We will revisit these subjects later to present a practical understanding and guide for the application of culture and mind-set as we unpack the strategies and tactics necessary to selling in China.

Contradiction and Paradox

We refer to China as a collection of markets rather than a single market not just because a country this large cannot be approached all at once. There is great regional, generational, and psychographic diversity. It's true that there are some quintessential Chinese values and traits. It is true that from province to province, city to city, and year to year, modern China's contradictions and paradoxes are profound.

These paradoxes apply most directly at the level of commercial systems—different segments of consumers have different tastes and behaviors, of course. But the widest contradictions concern the landscape for actually getting your product into a market. A few *ko'ans* about modern China:

- It is very rich and very poor; very modern and quite backward.
- It is hypercapitalist in some places, still very Communist in others.
- The government is always present and controlling, except when it isn't.
- It has super-developed consumers and many who still merely subsist at a material level.
- China, in some places, is the epitome of natural wonder and cleanliness and it has some of the most polluted places on Earth.

The mind-set is the precondition for getting past the confusion that contradictions cause. Remember, you're in a different ecosystem, so check your assumptions. One example: A bedding textile company in the United States hired Tompkins to provide it with a comprehensive analysis of the bedding market in China and to provide it with an entry and growth strategy. It specialized in blankets and bedding made from fleece and was very successful in the United States.

While our research showed massive growth in the bedding products category in China, within a week we realized that the company could not enter China with its current products and business model for several reasons.

- **Practical:** China has only a 2 percent penetration rate for dryers. The vast majority of Chinese air dry their clothes and bedding. Fleece would take almost two days to fully air dry.
- **Belief System:** Chinese people believe that fleece or any other non-natural fiber is bad for the skin, bad for health, and poses a particular threat to children.
- **Traditional:** Blankets made up only 2 percent of sales of all bedding in China. Almost all Chinese use a heavy comforter and a sheet, but no blankets.

In the end, we used this information—based on history, culture, and mind-set—to determine the needs and purchase motivators of Chinese bedding consumers and created an alternate model and product mix for entry.

Therein was the Chinese paradox: It's the fastest growing bedding market in the world, but some products were a no-go based on superstition and lack of dryer penetration. This did not mean our client could not succeed in China; in meant it needed to think and act in Chinese.

Summary

- China's super consumers did not emerge from a cultural void, or from a culture similar to our own, but from national and regional cultures that have developed over a 4,000-year period. Accepting that modern China has grown and been shaped by its own long-established patterns and logic is the first step to seeing China and its consumers as they really are.

- Purchase triggers for Chinese consumers have to be developed to work with the deep values of the target audience. A marketing program for Japan or Korea is as irrelevant as one from Brazil or Australia. A program for Beijing will not necessarily connect in Guangzhou. Market research data from China that resembles a past stage in your home country's development does not imply the same market, channel, or product-development process. Check your assumptions about development at the door.
- All of the above must shape your strategy for branding, merchandising, pricing, rewards, channels, colors, sizes, and operations.
- An understanding of history, culture, and mind-set must be coupled with an understanding of modern China's contradictions, paradoxes, and realities on the ground.
- Market opportunities—for example, concerning partnership and distribution, pricing, and channel strategy—must be approached in the circular Chinese way, not always in the Western linear way.

CHAPTER 3

A Self-Contained Empire

Study the past if you would define the future.

—Confucius

Now we begin our quick and targeted tour of history: four millennia of backstory, highly condensed for its relevance to China's super consumers. As you read these short chapters, remember two incontrovertible facts: China is really big and really old.

The more you work with China, the more meaning and relevance you'll see in those simple truths. Modern China has grown from its own logic, from its own long-established patterns. It's true that China's super consumers are especially receptive to brands, especially intrigued by what brands mean, and particularly willing to spend extremely large amounts of money on consumer goods. But this behavior is not simply the result of marketing skill. It's the result of bringing Western-based marketing skills into a perfect storm: just the right time, conditions, and psychology.

Americans tend to call Europe and the places their ancestors came from the Old Country. When compared to China, though, the 1,400-year history of the English monarchy looks positively fresh—and

America's 250 years? A mere blip. Among the reasons why Americans see China's economic power as a new phenomenon:

1. America does not have immediate neighbors other than Canada and Mexico. Further, it is a young and huge nation, bounded by two oceans. As such, America is so self-referential that it does not really have a mainstream collective memory of the history of nations other than the ones that its dominant population came from.

2. The New World—a North America colonized by Europeans—did not exist during China's previous peaks of global economic power, The Silk Road Era (Tang Dynasty), the Monogolian world conquest (Yuan Dynasty), or the height of the Qing—China's final imperial dynasty. From the time of our colonial period through our Civil War, China was in fact something of an obsession for the British Empire. It ended with China having so much economic power over the British Empire that they went to war.

Then there is the other reason we tend to be less aware of China: It is itself a self-referential, continental power. There's nothing subtle in why the Chinese named themselves the Middle Kingdom (between Heaven and Earth).

For the vast majority of its history, China's outlook and focus have been inwards: looking in a mirror rather than through a window. The land, the culture, the rivers, and the people were all self-sustaining, and produced (for much of its history) the richest and most advanced civilization on Earth.

While the Egyptians built the pyramids and then let them crumble; while the Greek, Persian, Roman, Mayan, Aztec, Native American, and numerous ancient and modern European empires rose and fell; and as Judaism, Christianity, and Islam were founded and flourished, China hardly noticed. There were interactions between East and West at times before the nineteenth century, but for the most part the two worlds were separate.

China, for its own part, was very busy. The ancestors of the people of modern China survived countless civil wars that were won and lost, and then finally won numerous territorial conquests; prospered under the healthy reign of great emperors and collapsed under the tyranny of corrupt ones; outlasted droughts and famines; achieved technological and artistic greatness; and watched magnificent palaces and cities burn, taking centuries of cultural achievements with them.

In many ways, China was a self-contained empire, an insular and inward-looking nation and culture for most of its ancient and modern history. Unlike the Roman and Greek Empires, which were expansionist and colonizing in nature and need—which put them into contact and conflict with other cultures, languages, foods, religions, and lifestyles very different from their own—China's expansion, growth, and consolidation happened almost singularly within its own homogenous cultural, linguistic, and geographic spheres.

China's dynasties, wars, conquests, rivalries, and major historical events between 3,000 BCE and the present largely took place in the landmass that makes up Greater China (Mongolia, Tibet, Xinjiang, Hong Kong, and Taiwan).

This isn't to say that China has no neighbors. It borders 16 other nations, more than any other country. And it has waged war and carried out diplomacy over the millennia to establish the boundaries with these (at least) 16 different powers as well as nearly a dozen other maritime neighbors.

Throughout its history, when the Imperial Government of China looked outward, it meant:

- Dealing with the Mongolians and other nomadic and Turkic raiders to the north and northwest, and managing relationships with Tibetans and Manchurians in the southwest and northeast.
- Stabilizing the central Asia lands—contemporary Kyrgyzstan, Tajikistan, Turkmenistan, Kazakhstan, Pakistan all border China—to permit overland commerce with Arabian traders.
- Establishing tributary relationships with other East and Southeast Asian kingdoms, such as the historical precedents of modern Vietnam and Korea, Malaysia, and Sri Lanka.

How did the Chinese check the ambitions of their neighbors? The same way as every other nation—more advanced military technology. Plus one other secret and apparently very powerful weapon: gifts.

Demonstrating a civilization richer and more technologically advanced than any of its neighbors was a deterrent to the ambitions of China's numerous neighbors. The treasures of Chinese craft and industry, such as bronze and jade jewelry, silks and porcelain, lacquer, and the most exquisite metal wares became tools of diplomacy. The Chinese employed gifts to curry favor. Gifts—proof points of cultural superiority—were deployed at massive scale and with great sophistication throughout reachable Asia.

The first theme of the super consumers rooted in this history is an intense appreciation for material goods, especially when luxurious or very finely made.

Domestically, the government's brief meant managing agriculture, industry, military, water and land resources, education, and taxes—and also preventing rivalries from springing up in Inner China, the established settlements, towns, and cities surrounding the Yangtze and Yellow Rivers. China's first dynasty was established in 221 BCE, becoming the first government ruled by a self-proclaimed emperor who conquered all the lands he could know (rather than simply a king of a certain territory).

The First Emperor standardized weights, measures, currency, the width of roads, and the tax code. The dynastic system would last 2,100 years until the fall of the last emperor in 1911. There were countless civil wars, famines, droughts, floods, rebellions, and extended foreign campaigns.

Points of continuity throughout these two millennia include:

- Tolerance for varied spoken languages but use of one standard written language
- Government administration of commerce and agriculture
- A nonhereditary civil service system based on merit
- A bimodal distribution of wealth—a very small, educated elite and a large, illiterate mass
- A desire for lasting stability

In a general sense, China's long and magnificent history has been marked by long periods of stability and unity but often punctured by chaos and decline. Thrift is a well-known Asian virtue. Clearly, in a world prone to falling apart, nothing conveys security as well as cash, except gold and silver, that is.

Over the arc of history, the pendulum swings from chaos to prosperity. The urban standards of living during the Han, Tang, Song, and Ming Dynasties were far higher than anything known in Europe at the time. The amount of wealth accrued by the Song Dynasty elite is staggering by any measure—and so is their patronage of art and craft.

The second theme of history and super consumers: A sense that current prosperity is a natural phase of celebration. The state of affairs circa early 2000s—even to the configuration of government—is fully aligned with the arc of history, and is normal. The time of necessary thrift has passed.

Throughout most of Chinese history there has been a theme of self-confidence relative to the world beyond its borders. Understandably. As demonstrated so artfully and scientifically by Ian Morris in his brilliant book *Why the West Rules—for Now,* we can look at a 15,000-year timeline of development and living standards in China and the West and see that China was either equal to or ahead of the West for most of the past 4,000 years.

To summarize: With almost zero influence from the outside world China invented, between 500 BCE and 1500 CE:

- A written language that has endured largely unchanged for more than 3,000 years, which also served as the foundation of written language for later Asian civilizations in Korea and Japan.
- A type and method of agriculture that sustained a people and built a civilization.
- A system of traditional medicine that is still relevant and in use in numerous parts of the world.
- Paper—second century BCE.
- Moveable type—estimated at 600 CE (800 years before Gutenberg).
- Gunpowder—as early as 620 CE.
- The magnetic compass—approximately 900 CE.
- The bristle toothbrush—1487.
- Porcelain—608 CE.
- Silk.
- Tea and the teapot.
- Toilet paper.
- The noodle.
- The wheelbarrow.
- The ship's rudder.
- Cast iron.
- Fireworks.
- The horse collar.

- Hundreds of other useful tools and consumer products; hundreds of scientific instruments, farming tools, weapons of war, medical devices, and medicines; and pleasure-giving products of all shapes and sizes.

Interestingly, aside from silk, porcelain, and tea, the Chinese did not seek to develop international trade for these inventions.

A sense of confidence, it can be argued, also underly the willingness of China's leaders to import philosophies that they believed would strengthen China. A few examples of imperial invitations extended to foreign emissaries as teachers:

- Buddhism, which the Tang Emperor believed would add strength to the culture. There has been coexistence and cyclic official embrace of one or more of the three native spiritual practices: ancestor worship, Confucianism, and Daoism, in addition to Buddhism.
- Arabic numbers.
- Islamic banking practices.
- Applied mathematics and astronomy from the Jesuits.

We could add communist revolution (advisors imported from Russia in 1910s) and the World Trade Organization (accession applied for in 1990s) but that would be skipping an important point: In the modern era, beginning in 1500 CE, China gradually—and then dramatically—fell far behind the West on almost every measure of economic, scientific, social developmental, and standard of living measures. As European mercantile powers rose by building ships and seeking riches through trade, Europeans attempted to engage in trade with China. But at this stage, under the Manchu Qing Dynasty, China's self-confidence deteriorated into complacency. The Qing court was utterly disinterested in the world beyond its own borders as anything other than a source of cash exchanged for Chinese exports of tea, porcelain, and silk.

The quest to make China's people into consumers of European-made goods led to invasion, war, occupation, and exploitation of China by foreign powers—including America. Through much of the nineteenth and early-twentieth century China felt profoundly humiliated by the West and Western technology.

Now, a third contribution of history to the super-consumer phenomenon: China has been restored, and its people can proudly occupy a place never available to them before—as consumers of goods made or inspired by the world beyond its borders.

Thus, many centuries of relative self-sufficiency, low consumption, and thrift brings to shopping today the sweetness of delayed gratification—a delay that spans not the past 50 years, but the past five generations.

CHAPTER 4

The First Globalization

It has been said that arguing against globalization is like arguing against the laws of gravity.

—Kofi Annan, former Secretary General
of the United Nations

The enlargement of the East-to-West movement of people, goods, and ideas that started during the time of Alexander the Great, and that peaked with the Mongol expansion of the Silk Road, marked the first period of globalization.

After a relatively isolationist period (450 to 1000 CE) following the fall of Rome, Europe was weak in commerce, power projection, and standards of living—truly the Dark Ages—while China flowered and flourished as we have seen previously.

Europe began its reemergence as a center of the arts, science, commerce, and standard of living (though it would take nearly 500 years) by two important events, both of which would lead to European and Western dominance from about 1500 to the early twenty-first century.

The first was one of the bloodiest chapters in human history. Launched by Pope Urban in 1096, the Crusades were ostensibly efforts to retake the Holy Land from the Muslim conquerors who had ruled over them for 400 years, as well as an effort to stop Arab and Muslim expansion into Europe.

The truth was that the pope was contending with multiple crippling issues including war in Germany; conflict with France; a war with the

Holy Roman Emperor, Henry the IV; and the question of who had the right of investiture (appointing bishops), popes or kings.

A mass pilgrimage and/or war that would unite Europeans under the Christian banner seemed just the tonic to ease his queasy stomach.

The crusades brought European armies, ideas, foods, banking systems, and culture to the East—along with a 250-year trail of death, destruction, rape, fire, disease, and general wretchedness on a cross-continental scale.

But crucial to our story, the Crusades also brought new ideas—as well as long-dormant ones—back to Europe. In particular, the Muslim caliphs and the great Arab empires that ruled from India in the east, to Morocco in the west, to Mongolia in the north, and Egypt in the south preserved the ancient philosophies, sciences, and treatises on government, art, and science produced by the Greeks and Romans. They also made their own huge advances in science, art, metallurgy, governance, and a religion of their own.

Many of these old and new ideas entered Europe for the first time during the Great Crusades or reentered Europe after a long absence. Very few of these ideas flowed east to China. The great barrier made up of Afghanistan, India, the Steppes, and the Gobi Desert kept China isolated. West and East only met through the middlemen who traveled along the early Silk Road for many years.

Ironically, a lack of conflict between China and the West was a key reason for isolation between the two sides at this time. China's previously mentioned self-sufficiency and isolationist bent were others.

The development, expansion, and profound success of the Mongol Empire was concurrent with the later Crusades of the early thirteenth century, which led to the largest and most successful expansion of the Silk Road—essentially the Internet of its era.

The most critical result of this transfer of products, science, and ideas between West and East was—combined with a set of emerging European ideas about nature, God, religion, and man—that it helped lay the groundwork for the Renaissance and the Age of Exploration, which would ensure Western influence over most of the globe.

We could spend volumes cataloging how the West and China diverged from 1096 until 1400, but instead we will shine light on the split through the stories of two sea voyages that helped change the fates of East and West.

CHAPTER 5

Marco Polo and the Two Admirals of the Sea

Hark, now hear the sailors cry, smell the sea, and feel the sky, let your soul and spirit fly, into the mystic....

—Van Morrison

There is some myth and uncertainty regarding Marco Polo's travels and adventures in China, but there is no disputing that he was the first European to document in great detail the wonders to be found in the Middle Kingdom.

Marco Polo was born in Venice in 1254 to a successful and adventurous family of merchants. His father, Niccolo, and his uncle, Maffeo, became wealthy traders in Europe and Asia. Eventually, their travels brought them to the Far East where they joined a diplomatic mission to the court of the great Mongol, Chinese Emperor Kublai Khan, grandson of Genghis Khan. There, over several years, they became intimate with and advisors to the ruler of the largest empire the world had ever seen. They traveled back to Venice in 1269 and, almost immediately, they planned their return to China and the Khan.

When they set out in 1271, young Marco Polo joined them for the adventure. It took them four years of brutal travel before they reached Kublai Khan at his summer palace, known as Xanadu. By this time, Marco had absorbed the sights and sounds of the Middle East and Central Asia, but nothing had prepared him for the splendor and plenty of China.

Not long after his arrival, Marco Polo earned the admiration and trust of the Khan—so much so that he allowed him full access to his Empire and sent him as a special envoy all over Asia.

In total, he spent about 17 years in China. He provided most of Europe with its first glimpse and understanding of China. Previously, the connection between West and East in trade and ideas was buffered by the thousands of miles of the Asian land mass and several layers of middlemen who traversed it. Very few Europeans had set foot in China and none had documented it well.

Polo's book about his adventures and dealings in China set imaginations ablaze in Europe. It was the birth of the 2,000-year-old dream of trading with and selling to China. The book also helped inspire the explorers of the Age of Exploration, including Christopher Columbus, to follow in Polo's footsteps and find a sea route to India, the Spice Islands, and China.

The Two Admirals of the Sea

The Italian seafarer Christopher Columbus—sponsored by the king and queen of Spain—sailed for India in 1492. He sought a fast passage that would open trade and exploration in the East, only to land in the Eastern Caribbean. Despite his horrific relations with the native populations— what today would be called crimes against humanity (enslavement, genocide, disease, exploitation, kidnapping, and murder), and despite the fact that until his dying day he believed he had found the Western sea route to India and China, it was a seminal moment in the history of East–West relations.

After the collapse of the Silk Road and European defeat in the holy lands, the path to China for trade was still blocked. Polo's book inspired merchants and kings to find a way to trade with China. But as yet no European power would or could pass through the Middle East for direct trade—not unlike their Greek and Roman forebears.

It can be argued that the Age of Discovery and Western commercial dominance was born of a desire to sell products in China. Europeans realized that they needed a sea route to the East if they were ever to find a way to import much silk, tea, and porcelain from China—as well as the spices and cotton of India—and to sell to the untold millions to be found on those exotic shores.

The European Renaissance gave new life and vigor to European art, culture, religion, architecture, and most importantly, commerce. In Italy, Venice, Florence, and Genoa reached their peaks as commercial city-states. The Flemish region was the progenitor of the industrial revolution. England and France became great powers. Europe was reborn and reinvigorated.

But, it was this very rebirth that led to the desire for more commerce, more room, more land, and new frontiers. The population explosions and desire for wealth and knowledge that came of the Renaissance could not long be contained in Europe.

China was still a dominant world and regional power, albeit without much contact with the outside world. In fact, China had the chance to beat Europeans in the race for modernity and world dominance. But Columbus sparked the Age of Discovery as well as the imperial, religious, and commercial colonization of Europe, North and South America, Africa, and the Far East.

All of this ushered in a 500-year dominance of West over East. But almost 90 years before Columbus convinced the king and queen of Spain to finance his great voyage, one of the greatest seamen, explorers, and leaders of men in world history set sail on his own voyage of discovery. He was Admiral Zheng He (1371 to 1433).

It is almost impossible to overstate Zheng's abilities as a seaman, soldier, and intellect; his insatiable curiosity about the world helped China see further beyond its borders than ever before. Some Chinese maps of the time typified the closed nature of the Middle Kingdom in that they only showed China, surrounded by the oceans. Zheng He could and would change that, for a time at least.

Chinese to Arab trade during the fourteenth century increased and China's knowledge and curiosity about the world gradually grew. A situation developed where China traded with the Arab world but no further west, and the West traded with the Arab world, but no further east.

The Yuan dynasty sought to build a larger base of knowledge and trade around the world, but it was the early Ming Dynasty that engaged in the rare (for China) idea of territorial, commercial, and imperial expansion outside of its immediate sphere. During the early Ming Dynasty (1368 to 1644) questions and confrontations regarding borders, loyalties, and positions within the royal court were rife. In the midst of this tumult a young boy, hailing from what is now Kunming and descended from a prestigious Muslim family, was in the royal court of Zhu Di, Prince of Yan.

The young boy, as he grew, showed incredible acumen for military affairs, politics, intrigue, and scholarly pursuits. He soon became a favorite and trusted advisor of the prince. In the years 1393 to 1402, there were several internecine struggles for power within and outside the Ming Court. In 1402, Zhu Di, his army, and his closest advisor, Zheng He, marched into Nanjing and defeated a nephew who had claimed the throne. A few days later Zhu Di was proclaimed the Yongle Emperor and went on to become a major force for change and advancement in China.

Zheng He held several important senior posts under the emperor, but most importantly he was made admiral and embarked on the first of seven expeditions in 1405.

The Yongle Emperor wanted to dominate trade in the Indian Ocean, take foreigners as slaves and sailors, and to exact tribute from lands in Africa and Arabia as they had become more aware of the extent and wealth of these foreign realms.

Admiral Zheng's first voyage set sail from Suzhou in July 1405. It included:

- A fleet of 317 ships.
- Almost 30,000 men.
- Dozens of linguists, who were trained at a new academy in Nanjing just for the purpose of the trip.
- The largest wooden ships in history (to this day) ranging in length from 216 feet to 420 feet (a football field is about 300 feet).

He made his seven voyages between 1405 and 1435, visiting the Horn of Africa, Arabia, Brunei, Thailand, India, and Southeast Asia. Along the way, he and his soldiers, sailors, and scientists established trade with several kingdoms, exacted tribute from many more, and brought home new ideas about science, technology, and cosmology.

It seemed as though China was on a path to imperial domination highlighted by two-way trade with other Asian and African countries, kingdoms, and tribes. And it is not hard to assume that, soon after, these enormous fleets would have sailed beyond Africa into the Atlantic Ocean and may have been the first old-world explorers to discover the new world.

But that would not be the case. The Yongle Emperor died in 1424. His successor, the Hongxi Emperor (1424 to 1425), stopped the voyages, burned the fleet, destroyed all its records and cut off trade even with China's closest neighbors. Although his son, the Xuande Emperor (1425 to 1435) allowed one more expedition, Zheng He's mission was over. Chinese ships were restricted to coastal waters and China turned its gaze back inward.

During the next 200 years, the European Renaissance and Age of Discovery would turn the tide and history of global development, living standards, science, art, technology, and commerce on a course of Western domination. The West would rule for the next 500 years.

From the late fourteenth century until the late sixteenth century, Europe was reborn. The arts, science, philosophy, and new forms of religion flowered. The period gave the world Michelangelo, Caravaggio, Galileo, and Da Vinci in the arts. It gave new life and importance to the classical thinkers and philosophies of Greece and Rome. The Protestant Reformation changed the way much of the world worshipped God and conducted daily affairs. Humanism and secularism began. The foundations for modern science were laid.

Perhaps most importantly, a perfect storm of environmental, geographic, and human factors forced Europe to look beyond its borders for wealth and expansion. With the path to the East and its riches largely blocked, Europe looked westward. The discovery and settling of the New World per Webster's, the commercial activity, and the colonialism that followed spurred the growth of a Western-dominated world.

CHAPTER 6

An Insatiable Appetite

Even in the centuries which appear to us to be the most monstrous and foolish, the immortal appetite for beauty has always found satisfaction.
—Charles Baudelaire

While all of this was happening in the West, China continued to flourish in its own realm. The Ming and Qing Empires would sustain China as a regional power until the early nineteenth century. But still, the goal of selling the fruits of the Renaissance and the New World to China was out of reach. But, that does not mean foreigners did not try to sell to China. There were some brief successes, but the history of trade with China is one marked by China—when it felt like it—exporting and selling products abroad, but almost never buying products from the outside world, accepting only silver and gold specie in return for their luxury wares. Why?

- Throughout its history China has been focused inward due to its size, population, and self-sufficiency.
- For centuries China was the leading scientific and economic power in the world.
- China invented many of the tools and products we still use today, and for a long time felt no need to sell them or spread them to the rest of the world; it invented everything it needed to stay viable and healthy for thousands of years.

- The European Age of Discovery and Expansion had many economic and consumer implications and effects; discovering and desiring Chinese goods was one of them.

England, Spain, Portugal, France, and Holland colonized the New World and established lucrative new international trade routes and regimes. The economic, nautical, scientific, and commercial success of this new world order made Europeans wealthy. The result was a desire to buy the things they wanted and an increased desire to expand trade even further.

During the 1600s and early 1700s, Europeans established trade with Asia through a series of commercial ports, colonies, and massive trading companies (the Dutch East India Company is one great example).

Europeans now found themselves wealthier than they had been since the time of the Romans. The desire to trade with Asia only increased. Starry-eyed proto-capitalists and traders envisioned a world where Europe, the Americas, and Asia could be connected by trade and profits.

While trade during the 1600s and 1700s developed and flourished, it was largely a one-way street: Europeans could not get enough of Chinese silk, cotton, porcelain, and tea, but China only wanted gold and silver specie in return. This had the debilitating effect of depleting European treasuries of much-needed currency. Of course, it also blocked the establishment, let alone evolution, of any real trade.

As we have seen, there was an active trade between China and the West throughout most of recorded history. Products, ideas, and people moved east and west across the Asian landmass—through numerous intermediaries—from the time of Alexander the Great's conquests through the height of the Roman Empire and into the Byzantine era. These exchanges intensified during the Crusades and the early stages of the Silk Road era. Still the trade was largely one way, with the West providing coin and raw materials in exchange for exquisite Chinese finished goods, all through middlemen and middle-countries.

Even after the Mongol conquest of Asia and during the golden age of the Silk Road, through the explorations of Marco Polo, the expansion of Western colonial and imperialist-backed trade under the Dutch, Portuguese, French, and English—and even after Europe had proven it had an insatiable appetite for Chinese goods, there were still no buyers for non-Chinese goods in China.

This begs the questions: Were there actually consumers in China? Were there people who bought not only the things they needed, but useful things, pretty things, and things they wanted? Were Chinese consumers buying all the things invented and made in China?

And if there were consumers in China, and they did buy things beyond the bare necessities, it begs another question: Why was there no market for foreign products and goods among the leaders or the people of China?

Freedom Creates Wealth in the West

First, let's address whether there were consumers in China between 500 BCE and 1600 CE first: The short answer is *no*. By and large, there was no consumer class in China during this period. Of course there was virtually no consumer class anywhere in the world prior to seventeenth-century Europe.

Kings, aristocrats, military leaders, conquerors, and the very wealthy from ancient Greece to Rome; from the popes, Charlemagne, and Henry VIII in the West to the emperors, mandarins, shoguns, sultans, caliphs, and moguls of the East—all desired, made, and bought the best things in life. They were protoconsumers, but they were a very small part of any population. They bought and used products that allowed them to enjoy a lifestyle beyond the imagination of the average person. They were able to commission or buy the best that their counties, provinces, and kingdoms could produce. In many cases, and with few exceptions, they also traded with other empires, kingdoms, and peoples to enjoy the best things that others could offer.

As marketers are prone to saying now, "The rich around the world tend to behave more like each other than like their own people." A Byzantine emperor's palace would be adorned with gold and silver decorative items from across the Near and Far East. His table would feature spices, fruits, meats, and vegetables from across the Mediterranean Basin. And his palace walls were built from the cedars of Lebanon and Roman Travertine marble.

The shopkeepers, farmers, merchants, and laborers he ruled would be lucky to own two sets of clothes, some useful tools, and a few treasured personal possessions or heirlooms. This was true across Europe, Asia, and the Americas at the time. It was not until the middle of the sixteenth century and the beginning of the seventeenth century that Europe and its colonies produced the first nascent consumer class outside of the elites.

So was the Age of Exploration the dawn of the consumer class?

As Russell Shorto explains in his outstanding book, *Amsterdam: The Story of the World's Most Liberal City*, the riches produced by Dutch traders, the Dutch East India Company, and the merchants and entrepreneurs of Amsterdam's golden age produced what was arguably the world's first middle-class consumer society. The Dutch never had a system of kings and nobles dependent on peasants who rented the land. Rather, the Dutch worked together to tame the sea, build a city, and build a country. They were—by necessity—tolerant and accepting of each other, in order to accomplish major public works that would benefit society as well as individuals.

It was Dutch liberalism that allowed for the religious tolerance necessary to create a haven and destination for foreigners to work. The Dutch focus on individual liberty, along with the lack of a legacy class system, enabled the Dutch to farm, trade, and prosper in what became Europe's richest and most productive country for nearly 100 years. This system produced a middle class that bought jewelry, art, furniture, food, drink, and creature comforts that improved the standard of living and provided for comfortable homes infused with unique aesthetic.

To greater or lesser degrees, in other European countries, in American colonies, and in Eastern colonies, the same was happening. A focus on individual liberty and freedom of commerce—as well as the riches freedom produced—created protoconsumer classes that had never existed before.

CHAPTER 7

Opium, Imperialism, and Decay

All empires fall, eventually. But why? It's not for lack of power. In fact,
it seems to be the opposite. Their power lulls them into comfort.
—Max Barry

King George III of England sent a delegation to Beijing in 1792, led by Lord George McCartney, in the hope of increasing trade with Britain, establishing a trade port, and opening a permanent embassy in Beijing. The mission was an abject failure ending with the Qianlong Emperor sending a condescending and mocking letter back to the king, who was not pleased with the Chinese emperor's refusal to even consider allowing his subjects to purchase any British-made goods.

The British Empire was importing massive volumes of tea from China and was paying for all of it in silver. Lord McCartney was famously banished to the barren rock known as Hong Kong. Decade by decade, British imports grew and silver reserves dwindled. Exporting the fruits of the Industrial Revolution to the colonies replenished British coffers, but payment was not always in silver and the amount was never enough. At times there were concessions by Qianlong's successors. For example, very small foreign legations were allowed to build small warehouses on the docks in controlled districts. Clergy were allowed to enter and minister to the small communities of traders—be they Dutch, British, or Portuguese—in Formosa (now Taiwan), Canton (now Guangzhou), or Macao. But these were token measures, useless in a crisis of mounting proportions.

Opium and War

By 1810, the British needed a strategy to reverse the flow of silver; to find some miracle product that the Chinese would pay silver for. They found it in the poppy fields of their South Asian colonies: opium. Initially the Chinese court agreed to allow a small quota of opium imports, to be negotiated annually. Then it appointed distributors to deal with the "foreign devils" that shipped it into Canton to reach inland markets. Foreign imports were being allowed, but in a tightly controlled and experimental way.

Selling opium does carry inherent risks. As the population of users grows, it ceases to be merely a problem for an individual addict and his family; it becomes generally detrimental to society. By 1840, the volume of imports had skyrocketed. Given the general state of decline of the Qing government, the time was right for cultivating outrage. A shipment of British opium was set afire. Reparations were demanded by the British and refused by the Chinese. A British gunboat ignored the rules and sailed into an inland waterway. Things escalated and the British gunboats easily won the day.

A Century of Exploitation

Then the British won a treaty requiring outrageous war penalties and worse: the right to establish port settlements under British control on Chinese land. Other nations demanded rights to colonize on the coast also, and the so-called Treaty Ports were born. Among the better known: The British took Hong Kong and Guangzhou, while the Germans made Qingdao their base for trade and established a very fine brewery there. French and international (British, Russian, American, and other) concessions were constructed in a fishing village called Shanghai.

These outposts of foreign wealth and power on Chinese soil were not only symbols of China's decline relative to the West; they were instruments for the economic exploitation and cultural humiliation of China by foreign powers. In a climate of growing disintegration, bandits preyed on the powerless. Impoverished armies of beggars and bandits, organized under a leader claiming to be the brother of Jesus Christ, carried out a decade-long uprising called the Taiping Rebellion, in which millions were slaughtered. Foreign armies had to be called in to end it.

In the period from 1850 to 1894 foreign powers established, at last, the goal pursued by explorers and European kings for centuries: trade between China and the West. In these decades, China had its first experiment with consumer markets, although these markets served only small populations, such as foreign residents and the Chinese traders who worked with them. A century later, these coastal cities would become the testing ground for a new era of trade and market liberalization.

Back to the nineteenth century. During this time, precious little of the trading wealth fed a domestic market. Customs duties, banking fees, and marine-cargo insurance policies all represented revenue for foreign companies. Foreigners controlled China's port cities. They had their own police and their own courts as well as separate generators and water systems; and they sheltered missionaries and criminals within their boundaries, beyond the reach of Chinese authorities.

These Treaty Port years were the death throes of the Qing Dynasty. Its fall can be attributed to many causes, but the most concise diagnosis may be, simply, failure to modernize. Not all Qing elites were blind to the extent or cause of decline. In fact, in the years from 1880 to 1899, the Qing Prince Guangxu sponsored a group of reformers who sought to bring modern military, education, and political systems to China. Though the 99 Reforms advocated studying Western technology—to borrow what was useful and ignore the rest—they were presented to the Empress Dowager as self-strengthening. One of history's great cultural chauvinists, the Empress Dowager had the prince jailed for treason in 1899.

Twelve years later, the Xinhai revolution of 1911 overthrew the moribund Qing Dynasty. Pointedly, the major source of financing for the revolution was the Chinese in America. The children of the men who built America's railroads heard the fervent pleas of a Guangdong-born, Japanese-educated doctor named Sun Yat Sen, who spoke of democracy. In time, the Nationalist government, led eventually by the Kuomintang Party (KMT), inherited the mantle of political control that the Xinhai revolution had wrested from the Qing.

Meanwhile Japan had signed up for the modernization program that the Qing Dynasty shunned. Japan's Meiji Restoration of the late nineteenth century brought confidence and wealth to the islands that were brought to the world's attention with victory in the Russo-Japanese war of 1904–1905, which was fought over imperial aspirations for both in regard to Manchuria and Korea. Emboldened by his nation's growing prosperity, Emperor Hirohito sought to expand the land mass under Japanese control. First through treaties, then through outright invasion and occupation, Japan took control of Northeast China. In the years from 1899 to 1927, Manchuria's rich agricultural land became the breadbasket for Hirohito's armies. One by one, the cities of Manchuria—Dalian, Changchun, Jinan, and Shenyang—became industrial bases for Hirohito's war machine.

The KMT, seeking military aid to combat the Japanese occupation, became a client state of the United States. The KMT paid occasional lip service to Christian ideals and secured millions of dollars in American aid. Unfortunately, the Nationalist government was also a glorified warlord regime: corrupt, violent, and willfully ignorant of its people's suffering.

End of War—Continuation of War

While the United States defeated the Japanese and ended the occupation of China, it was to be another foreign ideological import—Communism—that finally ended imperial and warlord rule.

In part, the Communists gained legitimacy and popular support by fighting more actively against the Japanese occupation than the Nationalists. When the civil war resumed in full between the two sides in 1945, another four years of bitter fighting for the future of China lay ahead.

When the Communists finally won, and the Nationalists fled to Taipei in 1949, Mao established a new government to preside over the rebuilding of a nation shattered by 100 years of warfare and exploitation.

Understandably, sensitivity over foreign involvement in China's economy persisted for some time following the establishment of the People's Republic of China.

In psychological terms, China had a very bad experience with the West, during which it lost power, prestige, territory, and its self-confidence. In practical terms, China's infrastructure—banks, roads, schools, and factories—was wholly inadequate as a foundation for a mid-twentieth century state, never mind a consumer economy. Then there was the issue of ideology. Clearly, if there were going to be consumers, let alone super consumers, they would have to wait for the wheel of history to turn another cycle.

CHAPTER 8

The People's Republic

A revolution is not a dinner party, or writing an essay, or painting a picture, or doing embroidery.

—Mao Zedong

Defeat in what Americans call the Pacific Theater of Word War II and what Chinese call the War of Resistance against the Japanese—in which the Communist fighters are the heroes—forced a Japanese withdrawal from China in 1945. For four more years, civil war between the Communists and the Nationalists raged. Then on October 1, 1949, when the Nationalists fled to Taiwan, Mao Zedong stood atop the Gate of Heavenly Peace—the entrance to the ancient domicile of the emperors (the Forbidden City)—to pronounce the founding of the People's Republic of China.

It was the symbolic and manifest end to a long period of decline, decay, dismemberment, and disruption in China. Mao claimed that China had now stood up. But to what end? The nation was on a new journey, but one that would not track directly to the goal of regaining its traditional place in the world economy or regional political prestige.

As much as 80 to 90 percent of China's population was rural. The country produced little in the way of machinery, vehicles, technology, consumer goods, or most of the time saving and lifestyle-improving products that, by this time, the West and much of the rest of the world were taking for granted.

Washing machines, refrigerators, modern stoves, and other common household goods were unheard of outside major cities and still rare in them. Carts pulled by donkeys were the dominant mode of transportation and ox-drawn plows were the primary agricultural implement.

Mao and the rest of the leadership were well aware of how far behind China was from the rest of the world in terms of industrialization and modernization. China had essentially missed out on the Industrial Revolution. As Mao stood at the Gate of Heavenly Peace, many of China's people lived in 1949 much as they had lived in 1749.

The New China

The first thorough reorganization was land reform. In rural China, Communist party members organized tenant farmers to overthrow the landlord class. Land became property of the state, but each farmer was given an allotment of land to work as the entitlement of his family and for the collective sustenance of the village. Decades later, as ideological battle lines escalated in the late 1960s, land reform escalated into large-scale collectivization of land into communes.

The second initiative was class struggle. In what must be the largest-scale episode of masochism in human history, for 30 years the Chinese people subjected themselves to relentless self-criticism, betrayal of their loved ones, and other campaigns of ideological purity. Mao drove the Chinese people to self-sacrifice for the national good and the good of Communist triumph. The system of class background was an ideologically rigid application of affirmative action, in which the poorest farmers were deemed the worthiest of all Chinese. Other classes were ideologically suspect in proportion to their material security and experience with the West. Interestingly, this phase—from 1950 to 1980—stands as the only era of Chinese history in which the official doctrine held that prosperity was equated directly to moral unreliability. At all other times from antiquity, China's leaders would uphold wealth as a social good. Moreover, no mainstream spiritual tradition in China has ever stood in judgment of the rich.

The third major initiative was industrialization, but of a productivist nature as opposed to consumerist. Industrialization was based on whatever China needed to be self-sufficient. Upon the ideological basis of providing for the basic needs of each person, China established a system of producing entities. Whether producing towels, motorcycles, light bulbs, or canned tomatoes, each factory had its trading arm to exchange with other producers. Each producer was a work unit that provided housing to workers and their family members, and that also distributed ration coupons for grain, milk, meat, and eggs, as well as towels and soap.

Initially the Soviet Union stepped in and provided vital guidance, materials, best practices, and infrastructure—a socialist Industrialization 101 effort. By 1958, however, the tensions between Beijing and Moscow had escalated. Taking things to a point of no return, Mao labeled the Russians "revisionist traitors of the revolution." The split was never mended. In 1989, 31 years later—as the Berlin Wall fell and the Soviet Union collapsed—China held to its judgment of the Russians as great teachers of what not to do.

Especially after the split with the Soviet Union in 1958, the economic policies of New China were based in fervent xenophobia. Self-sufficiency became the rallying cry. China's government would provide the Iron Rice Bowl, giving each and every Chinese citizen all that he needed (in theory) and none of what he wanted.

In many ways, New China was the familiar phase of isolation redux. Zheng He's fleet burned. Lord McCartney was rebuffed. Reformers were imprisoned by the Empress Dowager. In times of great prosperity and great difficulty alike, the Middle Kingdom has a record for trying to make the rest of the world go away. So, with an economy that had to be started almost from scratch the Chinese people had not the time, the leeway, nor the ideological permission to be consumers. Because there were many triumphs and positive outcomes in the early years, women were freed from chattel status. Public health systems were established. The writing system was simplified, literacy rates skyrocketed, and technical institutions were built—an emphasis on science and engineering developed generations of talent to build the country. China got its nuclear bomb, and the threat of invasion ended. The nation's industrial, economic, and physical infrastructure greatly improved and the people's standard of living was enhanced in a number of key ways. Yet the chaos of class struggle still prevented a sense of security in daily life. The stage was set for China to emerge once again. But not before the Great Leap Forward and the Cultural Revolution would lead to 30 years of struggle, suffering, and ideological purity over pragmatism.

CHAPTER 9

The Mandate of Heaven

Zhong Guo is Chinese for the country we call China (as rendered in Pinyin Chinese, written in Arabic letters); it translates as "the middle place," "middle country," or the "Celestial Empire between heaven and earth."

For thousands of years Chinese emperors (and their subjects) believed that a leader was not only a son of heaven, a divine being honored and obeyed as such, but that his position and right to rule was mandated by heaven (*tian*). The mandate did not have time limits, it did not decree that a ruler must be of noble birth, or even be of Han Chinese origin. The emperors of the Yuan (1271 to 1388) were Mongols, and the Qing (1644 to 1912) emperors were Manchus.

But there was one very important condition. The mandate was contingent upon an emperor ruling in the best interest of the country and its people—at all times acting in a just and righteous manner. Chinese ideals, even before Confucius, stress order from the top down as a paramount condition for harmony on earth. Those below must obey, but those above must be exemplars of righteous conduct. Failing to act as those exemplars would bring bad harvests, widespread poverty, instability, and natural disaster. The mandate from heaven could be withdrawn based on bad behavior. The dynasty would fall. Chaos and misery would reign.

Across some 3,000 years, the cycle repeated. For a time, an emperor and his successors could enjoy the Mandate of Heaven, impose their will on Chinese life, landscapes, cities, armies, neighbors, friends, enemies, and history. Until, inevitably, they didn't anymore, and the cycle would begin anew.

The residents of Tangshan, a medium-sized, working-class city in Hebei Province, northeast of Beijing, went to sleep the night of Tuesday, July 27, 1976, in their work-unit residences or collectivized farms. After eating at the canteen they likely listened to the radio, or played badminton or cards. They were ready for sleep after work in the fields or at their work units. They took buses, biked, or walked home in their navy, green, or gray pants and summer-weight T-shirts. They expected to wake up and head off to another hot day of work.

In their hour of peace and rest, precisely at 3:42 A.M., on Wednesday, July 28, something happened that would alter the course of Chinese and world history. The earth began to shake, walls began to tremble, and then a thunderous explosion was heard. The shaking intensified. A massive hole in the earth opened up. Suddenly the world exploded and collapsed in on itself like a supernova. Soon everything, including people—for miles in every direction—was broken and buried in dirt and ash, like a modern approximation of Pompeii.

It registered a 7.8 on the Richter scale and lasted for an unusual and hellish sixteen seconds. In the first five minutes, more than 150,000 people died. Sixteen hours later, a 7.1 magnitude aftershock hit and another 100,000 souls were extinguished while untold numbers were injured and made homeless.

Whatever was left of Tangshan and the surrounding countryside after the initial earthquake, collapsed into twisted metal, limbs, and dust after the second. It was the third-worst earthquake in recorded history. Some estimate that the actual death toll was closer to 500,000. No one will really ever know.

Because China had disengaged economically from the rest of the world in 1949, because it had broken off relations with its key ally, Russia, in 1958, and because once again the country had committed itself to self-sufficiency and isolation, there was little help from the outside to be had. The United Nations and countries that had diplomatic relations with the People's Republic offered aid to earthquake victims. China refused.

The quake had come seven months after the death of China's beloved Premier, Zhou Enlai. He was the ultimate martyr to his nation, a man who held the country together during the Cultural Revolution despite suffering enormously in personal terms. His death moved millions of people to Tiananmen in a national outpouring of grief: they wept, left flowers, and poems. The Gang of Four (Mao's last wife Jiang Qing and three other powerful party officials who held sway during the Cultural Revolution) hated Zhou Enlai and attempted to prohibit the showing of grief. But the grievers took it further. Not only did they leave poems for Zhou, but in a sign of things to come, they left little bottles—a homonym in Chinese for the name of another beloved leader: Deng Xiaoping.

It was not clear at the time, but the Tangshan earthquake was perhaps the moment when Mao's regime lost the Mandate of Heaven. It was the disaster that set China on a new course, one that would change the world. A few weeks later, on September 9, 1976, Mao Zedong—New China's founder, military leader, philosopher, and politician; the Chairman; the Great Helmsman; the icon—was dead.

Chinese history, tradition, and myth seemed to have stayed true to form. The great natural disaster, bookended by the deaths of China's two most important figures, ended the cycle, portending great changes. In the absence of Mao and Zhou—the firebrand and the caretaker; the great revolutionary and the great statesman—was a great vacuum, and not just of leaders to fill the top two posts. The scale of mourning for the dead and damaged of Tangshan—the loss of the Great Helmsman and the people's protector—was profound. All of the loss created space for something different. The question was: Would China seize the moment and set a new course?

Most, if not all, of Beijing's power elite knew that not only was the next generation of leadership at stake, but the future direction of the country's economy, the Party, and the people were at stake. The Great Leap Forward and the Cultural Revolution—along with a centralized command economy and collectivized farming—had failed to put China's economy in the world's top 5, or top 20 or top 50, even with the largest population on Earth. These movements had failed to restore China, a great civilization and a powerful nation, to fuller leadership in the world. Instead, the famines of the Great Leap Forward, the demonization of intellectuals during the Cultural Revolution, a third-world manufacturing infrastructure, and agricultural policies that disincentivized farmers to grow more left China near the bottom of almost every category of modernization, industrialization, and economic standing in the world.

Many in China's power structure thought the country not only needed new leaders but that it also needed a new system, a new soul, and a new way to stand up. Symbolically and materially, through omens of disaster and death, the stage was set for the inside struggle.

There were, of course, factions who wished to uphold adherence to Maoist/Marxist doctrines and practices. There were those who thought that the purity of the struggle had been compromised, and that given enough time and effort pure communism/socialism would prevail over democracy and capitalism.

Remember, it was 1976. Were not the Soviets giving the Americans a run for their money in the Cold War? Didn't Soviet Communism rule the eastern half of Europe? Wasn't the revolution triumphant in North Korea and Vietnam? Weren't countries in Africa consolidating and expanding Communist influence and rule? Across the Atlantic, Castro and other leftists in Central and South America were fighting and in many cases, winning the battle against the West. Even India's communist party reached its apex in the 1970s.

There were others though—those who had internalized the events of the past 30 years, the past 10 years, and especially the past year—who seemed to have realized that (as the saying goes): "The definition of insanity is doing the same thing over and over again and expecting a different result." There were those who asked, "What can we do differently?" "What can we absorb from prosperous nations, whether capitalist, socialist, totalitarian, or democratic, without losing our own identity?" They asked, "What can we do, within the autocratic framework of the Party, to improve the country?" They asked, "What can we do to ensure the Party remains in power while at the same time catching up with the Western World?" "Should China continue in isolation, realign with the USSR, create and lead a bloc of third-world nations?"

"What is it that all of our brothers in Communism/Leninism/ Maosim across the globe have in common?" they asked. The answer was they had the ideology, the doctrine, the dogma, and the will to fight. They were fighting racism, colonialism, exploitation, and the terror of wealthy elites imposing their will on the working class.

The only problem was that it had become harder to deny that the capitalist, democratic West was wealthy, which meant a higher quality of life, longer lifespans, and an infrastructural footprint that created options for future development, and—most of all—political stability.

To be clear, the reformers were ready to lead China out of poverty but not into capitalism. The priority of early reform—as in 1898—was to borrow technology from the West while avoiding its corrupting moral influences. We'll take highways, but leave the opiate of the people, religion; we'll import trucks but decline private automobiles. The goal was not to create a consumer society but rather to have enough prosperity and technical development to guarantee sovereignty, and moreover to assume a place of dignity and participation in global affairs—above all, to remain Chinese.

China wanted what it once had: wealth, well-educated people, regional prestige, and stability. To these men and women, the first order of business was to accumulate capital for development, to get rich as a nation, to rise peacefully on the world stage. Everything else would follow. Gradual, incremental, logical change that was compatible with stability, and a foundation for reclaiming greatness again—if it be China's fate.

Which was it to be: a doubling down on the Communist/Maoist system or incremental change that would provide a new path to power, wealth, and influence?

The factions and key players continued to struggle.

At first, in the wake of the purge of the radicals—led the Gang of Four—placing anyone but a Mao loyalist in his shoes as party chairman was highly unlikely. And so Hua Guofeng, whose ideology was essentially, "What would Mao do?" was placed in the post. Among his acts in power was the rehabilitation of a highly regarded, yet thrice-purged party veteran, Deng Xiaoping. The little bottles placed at Tiananmen to mourn Zhou Enlai had been seen. Not long after, Deng would rise and replace Hua as de facto leader of China.

It is testament to Deng's moral authority that in a nation with three central government structures—party, military, and state—Deng essentially ruled China from 1978 until 1992 without ever holding the top party or state titles, and he held the top military role for fewer than 10 years. It seemed that the Mandate of Heaven had been given to Deng and a new cycle had begun.

Opening and Reform

It was Deng who would provide the impetus, the spirit, and the determination that would lead to the changes in China forever memorialized and referred to as Reform and Opening.

By himself, and through his handpicked successor Jiang Zemin, Deng navigated the minefield that is the Chinese Communist Party and brought China to a watershed that changed the world. The politics involved are well beyond the scope of a book about consumers, but suffice it to say the events Deng put in motion set the stage for China to create the world's second-largest economy and to create the world's second class of super consumers.

Deng initiated the Reform and Opening movement with the theory of the socialist market economy, which he also described—with a nod to terms such as northern European socialism—as "socialism with Chinese characteristics." The socialist market economy would see China move from simply making things that made other things—steel, oil, and chemicals—and things that only had a utilitarian bent, to producing goods that could be consumed in and of themselves.

Take a moment to consider why Deng used those two terms, Reform and Opening. Reform meant that the central government would have to promote and accommodate change—specifically, the changes that would allow China to prosper. Reform never implied a rejection of socialism, the dictatorship of the party, or the Chinese cultural identity. It did imply that Deng would not indulge in unnecessary ideological scrutiny of methods that would reliably provide for the basic needs of the Chinese people.

Key and early domestic reforms included decollectivization of agriculture: allowing families and villages to develop their own systems for feeding their people. Tending their own plots and selling the excess at markets would protect farmers from the mass starvation of the 1950s.

Opening was the realization that China could not survive as a hermit kingdom. The country would need to allow foreign ideas, practices, people, and investments if it were to really stand up on the world stage—and if its people were to realize a standard of living comparable to the developed world. The experiment to allow foreign investment began with four special economic zones (SEZs). Shenzhen, across the land border with Hong Kong—which in 1985 was a tiny village of fisherman, smugglers, and prostitutes—was the most successful. Today, it is a megacity of 14 million people. The other three SEZs sought to tap the investment capital of overseas Chinese living in Taiwan, Thailand, and Macao.

Shenzhen did, in fact, attract mountains of Hong Kong investments. The then-British colony, with both manufacturing and finance industries, needed a hinterland. With tax holidays, preferential policies for hiring, flexible structures in leasing, and a pilot program for licensing foreign investors and bringing foreign capital into China, Shenzhen took off.

As the 1980s turned into the 1990s, the SEZs were proving to be a huge success and thousands of companies from around the world seized on the opportunity to make, produce, and procure Chinese-manufactured products.

It is important to note that the initial manufacturing model was not based on the Japanese model. The Japanese products that stormed the world markets in the 1970s and 1980s were, by and large, dreamed up and engineered in Japan—by Japanese people and companies, branded as Japanese, and exported to the world as Japanese products.

Chinese manufacturing on the other hand, from the start to the present day, is marked by foreign companies and people bringing their product ideas and designs to China for manufacture and assembly and then being sold under the foreign company's brand.

Green Shoots

Throughout the 1980s, as Reform and Opening was asserting itself, tangible changes in life in China were apparent. It was during this period that the first foreign brands, luxury items, and hotels began to appear. After struggles between conservatives and reformers and political struggles in the late 1980s, when the future of reform was in question, Deng Xiaoping toured southern China to assert that the reform movement would continue and that "a market economy with Chinese characteristics" was here to stay.

As the 1990s progressed, state-owned enterprises were being privatized on a massive scale.

Deng Xiaoping's two proclamations—"To get rich is glorious" and "It doesn't matter if a cat is black or white as long as it catches mice"—were now becoming reality. The pent-up work ethic and entrepreneurial spirit that characterizes so many Chinese was let loose. People were making things, both for export and domestic consumption.

"During this initial period of market-economy experimentation, consumption was still largely based on trade," notes Dr. Baohong Sun, a prominent professor of marketing at the Cheung Kong School of

Graduate Business in Hong Kong. "In the late nineteenth and early twentieth centuries there were a great number of homegrown Chinese brands of tea, medicines, food, beverages, clothing. China was not a consumer society in the modern sense but was a trade-based society. This activity was halted after 1949. In the early Reform and Opening era, this homegrown brand trade society started to reemerge and was an important step in the transition to a robust consumer society."

The more people made, the more money they had and the more they could buy; and the more they could buy, the more they wanted to make and buy even more things. Therefore, much like American super consumers, Chinese super consumers were born in the furious rush to industrialize, modernize, and make.

In the wake of a tragic event a system fell, a new one was established, and hundreds of millions of people began to prosper. The insatiable appetite to buy and the birth of a world-changing demographic was born.

CHAPTER 10

A Boom Is Born

Renee Hartmann and Sage Brennan have always been a little bit ahead of their time when it comes to China. Brennan first went to China in 1987 as a student who had become interested in all things Chinese. He studied the language, became fluent, and soaked in Chinese life and culture at a time when very few foreigners were even thinking about China beyond the term Red China—he listened, learned, and laid the foundation for what would become his life's work.

Hartmann began her career in finance and investor relations. She first entered China's business world and learned the ropes by advising Chinese companies seeking to go public on overseas stock markets. In 1999, she traveled to China to advise one such client on its plans to list on NASDAQ. During a meeting, the company's inside counsel asked, "We have heard of a term called *insider trading*, is this something we should know or be concerned about?"

After that experience, Hartmann saw an urgent need and opportunity for someone with her expertise in China. She moved to China in 2000, went to work for advertising and public relations giant Ogilvy and Mather, and started the first investor-relations practice in Mainland China.

As she was building Ogilvy's investor relations practice, Brennan was realizing the dream of his youth—living in China, where he was advising foreign companies on investments, market strategy, and technology projects with the leading technology consulting firm in Beijing, BDA China.

Brennan and Hartmann returned to the United States in 2003 to pursue their MBA degrees; Brennan at the University of North Carolina at Chapel Hill and Hartmann down the street at Duke University. Despite a number of other international job opportunities, they both wanted to return to China in order to participate in what had become a full-fledged boom—especially during the lead-up to the 2008 Beijing Olympics.

Upon returning to China, Hartmann cofounded a lifestyle apparel and footwear brand, called *eno*, with a group of former Nike China executives. At its peak, eno had 25 stores in first- and second-tier Chinese cities and was huge success. Her understanding of the Chinese language and culture, her particular insights into Chinese youth culture, and the lessons she learned for successful operations in China were key factors in eno's success. Perhaps most important of all, she found the perfect blend of the US original (street wear) and Chinification. Her decision to hire Chinese designers, who *knew*, literally and figuratively, their intended customers gave eno its competitive edge. It is remarkable that she, as a foreigner, could found a brand, open a store, secure $8 million in funding, expand to 25 stores, and find a successful exit. The timing was right as well. A consumer boom was being born just when eno opened its doors.

Hartmann and Brennan both started to see that Chinese consumer spending was maturing and growing exponentially, and that brand was the key driver for Chinese luxury buyers, outbound travelers, and growing middle class. This led the two, now married, to start a new company, called China Luxury Advisors, a boutique consulting firm that helps brands and retailers build and implement strategies for engagement with Chinese luxury consumers.

Over the course of their time in China, Hartmann and Brennan have had a front-row seat to the rise of China's consumer boom. Prior to 2000, consumerism in China was still in its early childhood—the boom barely existed beyond its infancy; it gained momentum in the early 2000s and, by 2005, it was in full swing.

To highlight the boom's evolution, Hartmann relates the story of how in its earliest stages Nike shoes in China were only sold in shrink-wrapped packages from under the counter at state-owned stores, such as Shanghai No. 1 department store.

"Consumers could not even touch or feel the product and would be served by surly ladies whose best feature was a scowl," she says. "This was the experience of China's first generation of emerging consumers."

A Boom Starts with a Swoosh and a Shot of Espresso

As Hartmann tells the story, "Nike realized it could never build a large-scale, sustainable business in the context of this onerous branding and retailing environment." There were, of course, issues with demand. "The fitness lifestyle boom, which Nike helped create in the USA in the late 1970s, had to be ignited in China. The company invested heavily to create demand—for example, building hundreds of basketball courts at Chinese schools—while simultaneously looking for retail models that could work within China's restrictive regulatory environment. In so doing, Nike pioneered China's retail industry, further fueling the resurgence of consumerism."

The starting point was State Council Proclamation 13. Early foreign investors in numerous sectors—from agriculture to aviation—needed strategists, negotiators, accountants, and lawyers in droves to find ways to work with the constantly evolving gray area of market access. Depending on which ministry or agency wrote which regulation or guideline at which time and place, investors could make an argument and then an application for investment approval.

Retail and distribution were not gray areas. No ministry or agency could develop a policy that directly contravened the State Council. And the State Council had declared, very simply "foreign participation in distribution and retail is prohibited."

As Hartmann explains, "The fact that Nike was producing high volumes of shoes and apparel in China, for export, did not mean it could legally sell any goods in China." A Chinese apparel or shoe manufacturer could, however, take to retail whatever they actually produced.

"The dominance of the single-brand retail format in China is a legacy of that legal structure. Underlying this legal structure was the interplay of various philosophies that have impacted the Chinese mind-set over centuries. First, the Confucian philosophy taught that agriculture, civil service, and crafts are noble activities, but trade is parasitic. Second, was Marx's Theory of Surplus Labor Value. That is, the adding of value to goods through packaging, transport, financing, branding, and retailing is inherently unnecessary. Given these embedded values, it is one thing to allow Chinese to earn money from trading and retail, but to allow foreign firms to control distribution and retail, to collect cash from Chinese consumers, and export their profits? That is another thing entirely."

In America, we may know nothing about the Opium War. But it's hard for victims to forget a century of humiliation, poverty, and a war that profited foreign companies and powers. In many ways, when China joined the WTO (World Trade Organization) in 2002—and allowed foreign companies to manage their own retail in China—it was proof that the country had finally regained its confidence relative to foreign economic powers. The exhilaration with which Chinese super consumers embrace foreign brands is a psychological echo of this reclaimed global power.

Back to Nike in the early 1990s: It had production and warehouses in China, and consumers in China who wanted its product. All that stood in the way of building a retail network was Proclamation 13. As a foreign firm that could not apply for a business license with a scope that included retail, distribution, or trade, what could it do? Indeed, it could do what every foreign brand that managed to get product onto Chinese shelves did: use two entity structures.

Hartmann elaborates, "One structure, known as the straw man, involved a Chinese private company licensed to buy and sell goods. Such a company would serve as the legal operator of Nike's single-brand store. These single-brand stores were located in department stores and sometimes stand-alone at street level, depending on the straw man's ability to secure a lease and negotiate terms. The cash collected from sales would go into the straw man's bank account. Obviously, there was a bit of a risk. What happens if the straw man decides not to hand over the money?"

Sage Brennan explains: "So Nike found a partner—in fact, several partners—to open Nike stores in a quasi-franchise, joint-venture basis. It might have been a cash risk, but it worked with consumers. Nike, which built its business through the expansion of key multibrand concepts in America, such as Foot Locker, found that the key to success was for Nike to control the product, the brand, and the experience."

This revelation may sound like Retail 101, but in the final decades of twentieth century China, it was revolutionary. Starbucks was another successful practitioner of the controlled-brand experience in China. It came in the late 1990s, later than Nike, but it used the same system. Working through three joint-venture partners—one in Guangzhou, one in Beijing, and one in Shanghai—the coffee chain built its brand by holding its partners to franchise-like terms of pricing, presentation, and service.

Brennan continues, "The second entity type gained popularity in the few years prior to WTO. In the manufacturing-oriented enterprise, or MOE model, manufacturers—even manufacturers with some foreign investment—were approved for business licenses that permitted sales of products that the entity had made. In this model, payment risk declined, because the foreign brand would control the bank account. Yet it was also not entirely audit proof. Nike could legally operate a few stores in Shanghai based on a production facility in Suzhou. But the goods made in Suzhou would never match up to the goods sold in Shanghai. That is, what single manufacturing location turns out shoes, running bras, T-shirts, and socks?"

Eventually, thanks to the WTO, the rules of retail ownership and operations in China were streamlined, and foreign companies could operate fully legally. By 2010, Starbucks had bought out its Chinese joint-venture partners and took control of its stores. Now, the major shopping streets and malls in every first, second, and third-tier city are lined with international brands, many of which no longer relinquish control of presentation—or cash—to a Chinese partner.

As Chinese consumers were increasingly introduced to foreign retail concepts—concepts from developed consumer economies—their desire to experience shopping grew, laying the groundwork for the coming consumer boom in China. The combination of a growing hunger for Western goods and services, together with loosening restrictions in retail, meant that thousands of new companies could enter China, which further fueled the consumer cycle. Choices and desire were on an infinite loop, feeding each other. A boom was born.

The boom was born in the early 1990s, when Opening and Reform allowed Chinese private companies to bring foreign-produced goods to retail. It expanded in the late 1990s as the legal models that worked around Proclamation 13 became commonplace. It intensified in 2002 to 2007, as WTO provisions to legalize foreign participation in retail took effect and foreign retailers responded. And it rapidly expanded after 2008, as the confidence and wealth of post-Beijing Olympics China found expression in conspicuous consumption. Today, Renee and Sage, through China Luxury Advisors, have used their 15 years of accumulated experience studying Chinese consumer behavior, operating retail outlets in China, and helping define the era of the China Global Consumer (more later) to help foreign companies understand their options in Chinese retail and to help them engage Chinese super consumers on a global scale.

Change at Hyper Speed

Having experienced it firsthand, and having helped dozens of companies enter and grow in China during this period, we can identify several trends and events that took China from a nascent consumer market to a consumer boom. These include:

- Mass urbanization
- The pent-up demand of Chinese consumers
- The myriad new choices for consumers
- New wealth, feeding the desire to display status
- Amplified exposure to Western brands and lifestyles through media, travel, and retail presence
- New rules and regulations regarding retail operations and investment
- Rapid entry and investment by hundreds of new foreign companies, willing to experiment with somewhat risky models
- China's admission to the World Trade Organization
- Increased sophistication on the part of domestic brands and retailers, which feed and serve consumption
- The surge in confidence by both government and the people following the 2008 Beijing Olympics

Luxury sales also started to skyrocket during the initial consumer boom, as premium brands and products were no longer the privilege of the few, but accessible and desirable to many. Three decades of urbanization resulted in pent-up demand for white goods and home furnishings. The ability to buy Western-style food and drinks, such as Starbucks coffee, Heineken beer, French wines, Häagen-Dazs ice cream, KFC chicken, and McDonald's hamburgers afforded the buyer with a sense of status and prestige.

Car culture also helped spark the consumer boom in China. As recently as 2002, bicycles, pushcarts, and scooters still largely dominated the streets of major Chinese cities. By 2007, auto traffic dwarfed other types of transport on city streets.

Virtually every consumer product, technology, and food and beverage company in the world now had to at least have a China plan on the table, whether ready for entry or not. Commenting on the change in consumer attitudes from pre-boom to boom, Hartmann notes that, "even as recently as 2006, for foreign companies it was all about education: educate the consumer, educate them on your products, on your brand's lifestyle, on how and where to shop. Then they started to spend, in record numbers. Now in many ways it has come full circle. Brands and retailers need to listen to and be educated by the Chinese consumer."

We agree that, in many cases, Chinese consumers are no longer content to simply buy whatever a brand has to offer. They are *telling* the brand what to offer, with the promise that if the brand can't deliver, they will move on. Chinese consumers have therefore become very brand aware, but not very brand loyal.

As Brennan puts it, "now you have world-class retailers and world-class shopping experiences in China. Many of the stores and flagships, run by the foreign companies themselves, are bigger, more glamorous, and better performing than their hometown originals. Additionally, you suddenly find world-class consumers. This has all happened in the last ten years."

The awakening of global companies to the potential of Chinese consumers, changes in government rules and regulations, rapid retail expansion, a new middle class and wealthy Chinese citizens, and the dream of making and spending a lot of money all played a role in igniting the Chinese consumer boom.

But, even then, it was hard to imagine that a boom would turn into a world-changing phenomenon and that Chinese consumers would turn into super consumers who would help shape the world in which we all work and live.

PART II

The Chinese Super Consumer—From Birth to Adolescence and Maturity

CHAPTER 11

From Sandpaper to Sephora—The First Super Consumers

When you have only two pennies left in the world, buy a loaf of bread with one, and a lily with the other.

—Chinese Proverb

In post-1949 China, women were discouraged from wearing makeup, *if* they could even find any. It was considered bourgeois and antirevolutionary for the typical female to try to make herself look Western or to stand out with rouge, eyeliner, or lipstick. After Reform and Opening began and this stricture eased, cosmetics were still extremely rare and hard to buy. Many women improvised by rubbing their cheeks and lips with sandpaper to give themselves the touch of red that would make them look and feel more feminine. In February 2013, Sephora—the wildly popular and successful French cosmetics and body-care chain—opened its largest flagship store in Shanghai, at the corner of Nanjing Road and Maoming Road. After opening its first store in China in 2005 and seeing steady growth and profits, it was clear that demand for multibrand cosmetics retailing was high and would continue to grow.

According to Sephora, the new flagship store has more than 1,500 square feet of sales space, spread over five floors, where Chinese shoppers can choose from 118 different brands (17 of which are Asian) and nearly 7,000 products. The store employs 100 people (out of 2,500 employees total for Sephora China). During more than a dozen visits to the store, we observed that it is almost always packed and traffic-to-sales conversions are high compared to other Western retailers in China.

How did the consumer who latently and instinctively wanted a fresh, healthy look—but had to resort to sandpaper—transform and mature into the consumer who could support 133 Sephora stores on the mainland? How did China go from sandpaper to Sephora in 30 years?

The story is a microcosm of China's transformation from ration cards and paper sandals to shopping meccas, rivaling Fifth Avenue, that offer virtually every product available in the rest of the world. China's super consumers evolved from non-consumers, to new consumers, to consumer boomers, to super consumers in a similar progression as that of the first generation of global super consumers.

American Century Redux

To understand the evolution of China's consumer revolution, it makes sense to look to the United States as a paradigm. When World War II finally ended, after six horrendous years on the European Front and after nearly 10 years in the Pacific, most of Europe lay in ruins. The English empire was a zombie, soon to disappear completely. While Russia was triumphant, it had lost more than 20 million people and had to rebuild its infrastructure while concurrently lowering the Iron Curtain across Europe.

In the East, Japan was reduced from a glorious and far-reaching empire to a humiliated, defeated, naked, and starving state. Much of Southeast Asia was destroyed and had to rebuild and reset for a post-colonial world. China would, after being rid of the Japanese, renew hostilities between the Nationalists and the Communists—and Korea was headed for civil war as well.

Standing alone after the flames and gore of the most destructive war in human history (more than 70 million dead) and physically unharmed, with an economy roaring from wartime production, was the United States. The combination of victory, economics, demographics, and a world on its knees combined to launch the American Century.

The seeds of the American Century were planted in the first wave of hyper-industrialization, during the pre and post–Civil War periods.

Major growth continued during the Roaring Twenties and the first era of financialization of the economy.

The Great Depression put a temporary halt to America's seemingly inevitable rise on the world stage, but with the end of World War II, the stage was empty of other actors, and the United States—for a brief period before the Cold War started—was left alone as an economic, industrial, and political power. Interestingly, the United States was, once again, left alone as a unipolar power after the end of the Cold War, and it was during this period that China's rise began in earnest.

But perhaps what most defined and propelled American exceptionalism and dominance in the 1950s, 1960s, and early 1970s was the birth of the American super consumer, the world's first such class of consumers.

With the war over, millions of G.I.s returning home, and no real competition, American industry produced the goods and services that millions of newly prosperous and growing families needed and wanted. The G.I. Bill educated millions of veterans and put them to work in education, technology, manufacturing, and services. Further fueling American industry and prosperity was the fact that manufacturing was crippled in Europe and Asia. The world needed American-made goods to rebuild. Even with global demand, it was the new domestic demand for material goods that created the American super consumer.

America's new middle-class super consumers went about the work of building new lives, new industries, and new frontiers. Postwar America was also the place where the world's first and largest mass-media movement developed. Radio expanded while newspapers, general interest magazines, and journals flourished; Hollywood found a new golden age but, perhaps most important, the introduction and rapid adoption of television changed the way Americans were informed, entertained, and marketed to.

Added to these two phenomena, a newly sophisticated, scientific, and all-encompassing approach to advertising and marketing emerged. The perfect storm of prosperity and need, mass media, and advertising created the largest spending spree and consumer class in the world's history.

The spending spree of the 1950s and 1960s was a reflection of age-old American ideals like individualism, freedom, self-expression, and a projection of new ones (suburban living, conspicuous consumption, status symbols). Millions of new houses were built as well and every manner of decoration, appliance, and entertainment equipment were made and bought to fill them. New televisions, radios, patio furniture, aluminum siding, and TV dinners; appliances, cosmetics, suits, ties, and shoes; transistor radios, food processors, furniture, and matching 12-piece sets of china. Americans bought pink flamingos for the lawn and toys for junior—in short, Americans were buying everything they needed and wanted when they wanted it.

Want. Need. Buy. Show Off. Keep Up.

There was a product for every real and imagined need or want in the America of the 1940s–1970s. But none perhaps loomed larger during the peak years of American super consumption than the car.

In 1956, President Dwight D. Eisenhower authorized construction of the Federal Interstate Highway System, and in fewer than 10 years America built 50,000 miles of highways. Detroit, flush with the profits of wartime matériel production, expanded and gave Americans, in 1,000 styles, sizes, and price points, the cars to drive on those roads.

American car culture was so deeply entwined with American postwar prosperity, freedom of movement, and consumerism, that even today—when we think of the 1950s—one of the first images that comes to our minds are big, tail-finned, muscular American cars pulling into drive-in diners and drive-in movies, and the new ritual of the automobile commute from suburb to city.

It was also at this time that American super consumers began to travel the world in astounding numbers. They went to Mexico, Canada, the Caribbean, and Europe. There were so many of them, with more money than experience that the image of the "Ugly American" loud in clothes and voices and with little appreciation or knowledge of other cultures was born. Houses, cars, vacations. The middle-class ascendant.

Super Consumption Goes Global

American super consumers not only changed their own lives and the US landscape; they also helped changed the lives, tastes, buying habits, dreams, and aspirations of people around the globe. At first America provided the world with what it needed, but increasingly, the world started to consume the soft-power products of America. People everywhere were exposed to and inspired by American lifestyle aspirations and aesthetics through movies, TV shows, music, and celebrities—these and other soft-power totems and icons made many want to look, talk, act, live, and buy like Americans.

Why not? Americans were seen as triumphant, powerful, wealthy, healthy, and happy. They were middle class, upper-middle class, upper class, and super wealthy. The false hopes of many poor immigrants, who, in the nineteenth century were told that the streets of America were paved with gold, were in many ways no longer false, but true. Even the poor in America were much richer than poor people in Asia, Africa, and Europe. The American dream was on display, and it was manifestly true to life.

American super consumers helped set the standards for consumption in the 1950s, 1960s, 1970s, and 1980s. They were spread globally, but not yet on an American scale. That is not to say there was universal appreciation for, or desire to, imitate Americans or that the possibility of doing so was feasible in many parts of the world. But enough influences spread to—ironically—Japan and Germany, the country's former foes, to help make them early adopters of postwar democracy, capitalism, and consumption. Others would follow.

Go West, Young Man

No matter what country, no matter how poor, no matter how different from America, no matter how free or oppressive the government, one thing was sure: Millions of people from hundreds of countries were inspired by American success, affluence, culture, and products to make them want to move to America or make their world more like America and to improve their comfort and well-being through consumption. Europeans, Asians, South Americans, Mexicans, and Middle Easterners came to America in the postwar years to take their chances in creating stable and prosperous lives for themselves and their families.

In some ways American super consumers helped strengthen America by drawing the brightest, most ambitious, and hardest-working people from around the world. The American dream said you could work hard, move up, make money, and spend it on anything and everything. While this was, sadly, not true for all Americans at the time, it was true enough for a majority of people to be attractive to outsiders.

A great example is Hal Zakkour, Michael's father. He was born in 1941, and grew up in Tripoli, Lebanon, one of 10 children. The Zakkours were people of modest means. What they lacked in creature comforts they made up for with family, food, love, and the beauty of living on the Mediterranean Sea with the mountains and the cedars of Lebanon at their back.

But with all that, there wasn't enough space, freedom, or opportunity for 10 kids to make it in this tiny state, smaller than New Jersey. There was also the inherent, ancient-Phoenician desire to move about and settle the world, to be merchants, to make one's way in trade and life. Hal Zakkour was lucky enough to be educated at an American-sponsored Episcopal school, where he played basketball and volleyball.

The first TV show he remembers seeing was *I Love Lucy*. At home, he listened to Elvis, Buddy Holly, and Richie Valens on the radio. On the corner with his friends he wore Levi jeans, a white T-shirt, and Ray-Ban–like sunglasses. Upon high school graduation in 1960—with the seeds of American soft power planted in him—he packed his few possessions and emigrated to America.

He worked low-skilled jobs in Miami to support his college education, earning an aeronautical engineering degree from Embry–Riddle Aeronautical University. He moved to New Jersey in 1964 and went to work for AT&T as an engineer. Eventually, Hal met Cynthia Maurizi, the daughter of Sylvester and Grace Maurizi, of Lodi, New Jersey, son and daughter, respectively, of the Maurizis and Maricondas, Italian immigrants who came to America in 1894 and 1895 for many of the same reasons Hal did in 1960.

They married, had Michael (and 18 months later Donna), and started to live the American dream. Ambition, hard work, and clean living produced a life with all of the needed and many of the desired things, a nice house in the suburbs of New York, cars, vacations, good educations for the kids.

So inspiring was the result that, in the mid-1970s, Hal's three younger brothers came to America and all three have built and lived the same American dream, the allure of which was enhanced and put on display by the nexus of American consumption, technology, media, and soft power to Hal Zakkour in 1958. And in a powerful illustration of the way that American super consumers changed the world, by attracting those who wanted to earn and spend like them, Michael grew up to write this book and now there are more than 50 Zakkours living in New York and New Jersey. All of them are successful professionals, engineers, corporate executives, business owners, traders, all of them with loving families, all of them buyers and creators of the American dream and the American promise of "Make and spend and ye shall be set free."

Lest anyone think that American consumption no longer takes center stage in America, remember that, for better or worse in the days after 9/11, President George W. Bush implored Americans to "go out and shop" as the way to support America in crisis.

America provided the world with its first super consumers and, almost 50 years later, China would produce the world's second super consumers, whose effect and influence on the world is and will be even more dramatic than the first.

China's Own Postwar Boom and Birth of the Chinese Super Consumer

On the scale of human development, China's super consumers have advanced, over the past 20 years, from birth to toddlerhood, to childhood, and now on to adolescence. Without even having yet reached adulthood they are changing the world, and they will only grow in numbers and influence in the coming years. "You cannot be a global brand and ignore Chinese consumers," says Dr. Ann Lee, a professor at NYU, author of the book *What America Can Learn from China,* and a keen observer of how Chinese consumers are altering the world order. "In fact, you have to make them a top priority or risk no longer being relevant globally."

But, what and who *are* China's super consumers? In a sense they are quite similar to their American counterparts. The seeds of their growth were planted in an earlier era. In this case it was the period between the abdication of the Last Emperor, Puyi, and the founding of the People's Republic. Just as the seeds of American super consumerism were planted in the post-Civil War and Roaring Twenties eras.

When the Republic of China was founded by Sun Yat Sen, England was at the height of its Edwardian power. European and American merchants, traders, and manufacturers were active in Shanghai and elsewhere, spreading the gospel of consumerism, capitalism, and—it must be said—hedonism. In these 20-some years, under the Kuomintang (KMT) government, China's most affluent citizens in China's most developed cities enjoyed the finer things in life, including imported goods. It was during this period that Shanghai came to be called the Paris of the Orient.

"From the mid-nineteenth century into the 1940s, Chinese business people, merchants, and retailers created brands, differentiated their products through marketing and regional cachet, and created distinctive packaging to entice consumers to buy their products," notes Professor Sun Baohong of the Cheung Kong Graduate School of Business. "There was a nascent consumerism that emerged from the death throes of the Qing Empire period."

In Shanghai, Canton, Tianjin, Qingdao, and other open cities where foreigners lived and traded, local Chinese businesses also learned about and absorbed the nuances of Western-style consumer product creation and sales, retail merchandising, and marketing. The first limited liability companies in China were founded in the late nineteenth century, breaking not only a pattern of millennia in which companies were either state-run monopolies or family businesses, but also challenging the Confucian stigma on trading and commerce.

The result was that urban Chinese on the eastern and southern coasts of China—through a combination of exposure to Chinese and Western products and brands, products, advertising, materialism, and living—became the first true consumers in modern Chinese history. For the first time, many Chinese outside of the power elites had the money and desire to buy things they wanted, not just needed, and had a wide array of local and foreign companies to serve their desires.

But the miseries of the Japanese invasion, the collapse of the Republic, and the escalation of the Civil War between the KMT and the Communists, quashed China's young and promising consumer culture and ushered in a long era of military, political, cultural, and spiritual struggles. Much as the Great Depression and World War II put America's path to hyperconsumption on hold, Chinese consumerism was put on hold—not for 10 years, but almost 70.

The collapse of the Qing Empire, Western imperialism, civil war, the Japanese occupation, and more civil war, were devastating for China and produced what many call the "100 years of humiliation" or "100 years of weakness." It was a time where China became weak, poor, and backward.

The founding of the People's Republic of China (PRC) in 1949 marked the end of this era and the birth of the new China. This was the start of China's first postwar period, from 1949 to 1979. While the PRC government ended war and raised literacy and life expectancy, it did not create the watershed for prosperity and consumer culture experienced by the United States in the 1950s.

It took another 40 years—30 years of a centrally planned economy and 10 years of experimentation and uncertainty about market economics—to plant that seed in fertile ground and to confirm that a market-style economy would be a firm policy commitment. At last, in the 10 years from Deng's Southern Tour in 1992 to WTO implementation in 2002, the super consumer was born.

In the Beginning

Chinese consumers began to engage with foreign products and a market-based system in the mid-1980s, when consumers could only buy foreign goods from a few specially designated, state-owned stores.

Eventually the rules were loosened and Chinese companies were allowed to set up privately owned entities to sell domestic and foreign goods. Pivoting off this model's success, the Chinese government then started to allow foreign companies to enter into joint ventures to sell products in a retail environment, whether through stand-alone stores or through other sales channels. Finally, the central government allowed foreign retailers and brands to operate on their own in China.

During this progression, Chinese consumers were exposed more and more to practical, utilitarian, fashion, and lifestyle products from around the world.

Some of the earliest entrants into the market were European luxury brands like Louis Vuitton and Ermenegildo Zegna, as well as big, American, fast-moving consumer goods (FMCG) companies like Procter & Gamble, Kraft, and Colgate-Palmolive. Other early movers included food and beverage giants like Coke, Pepsi, and Yum! brands. In the 1980s and 1990s, the regulatory environment was difficult and unknown terrain; distribution and sales were limited; costs were high as well.

In these early years, however, virtually no foreign brands—regardless of product category—were making money in China. Rather, these brands believed in the promise of China; they took the long-term view that in 5 to 15 years, Chinese consumers would have the disposable income to buy their products.

The difference between the consumer boom years and the era of the China super consumer is most dramatically marked by the fact that not only the market of 400 million in coastal China are your potential customers, but that consumerism and consumer products have penetrated all of China to one degree or another. With the exception perhaps of only the most desperately poor, even low income and rural citizens are consumers. A subsistence farmer can still be found using P&G toothpaste, drinking a Coke, and applying domestically made cosmetics.

The big winners from 2000 to 2014 were the companies that entered early, absorbed losses, learned the market, and—most important of all—built mindshare and brand loyalty through major investments in marketing, merchandising, and physical plant. Those that are succeeding today and will succeed in the future with Chinese consumers will build on past lessons learned, ask Chinese consumers what they want, understand that they are a global as well as local demographic, and engage them on their own terms.

With this background we can answer the question, "What is the China super consumer?"

- The second-largest and potentially largest consumer class in the world (by numbers and dollars spent).
- Already leaders in consumption of select product categories.
- Have taken some cues from American and other Western super consumers, but their psychology, desires, and purchase motivators are Chinese.
- Still in the adolescent phase—trying to define themselves; changing their looks and habits frequently. They are still somewhat fickle; but are also full of vitality, vigor, and energy.
- Changing the ways business is conducted around the world, whether companies are consumer product, business to business, or technology.
- Will be the largest, contingent, and most free-spending outbound traveler in the world by 2020.

- Already account for 25 percent of luxury-good sales globally, and spends 60 percent of that outside Mainland China.
- Brings change to the natural environment in China and abroad.
- No longer defined by the companies that want to sell to them, Chinese super consumers are defining themselves.
- Served by a mix of foreign and domestic Chinese companies and his or her preferences will make winners or losers out of many of them.
- A game-changing global demographic, not just a market.

CHAPTER 12

The China Market + The China Global Demographic = China's Super Consumers

Thirty years ago, if you had a choice between being born a genius in Bombay or average in Poughkeepsie, you would have chosen Poughkeepsie, because your chances of enjoying a decent life were greater there. Now, in the new plugged-in, interconnected, flat world ... I would rather be a genius born in China than an average guy born in Poughkeepsie.
—Bill Gates

What is the China market? How do we define it? Is it a place? Is it a group of people? Or is it like ancient Rome—an idea, a dream?

We start by first recognizing that there are three definitions of the China market, and all three have played a role in the creation and continuing growth of hyper-consumption.

1. **China.** China is a continent-sized country with a population of approximately 1.3 billion people. Among the few traits shared by the majority of people across China are its written language and the fact that about 90 percent of the population is made up of ethnic Han.

For all but a few brands and companies, selling nationally in all of China is nearly impossible and not necessarily desirable.

2. **Coastal China.** Coastal China is made up of a string of cities and provinces that start with the capital in Beijing, in the northeast, running down the east coast through Shanghai and the major commercial and industrial cities of Jiangsu Province (Suzhou, Changzhou, Nanjing, Wuxi), further south into wealthy Zhejiang Province (Hangzhou, Ningbo, Wenxhoi), and down into Fujian Province. From there, a sharp turn to the west brings you along China's southern coast and the mega-cities of Guangdong Province (Shenzhen, Guangzhou, and Dongguan) as well as the Special Administrative Region—Hong Kong. Coastal China is a country within a country. It is the most financially developed and wealthy portion of China. It has the most experience in market economics and consumption, and it is the place where most foreigners visit, live, and conduct business. In short, it is the place where, for the last 15 years, China's consumer boom took place and where the Chinese super consumer emerged.

3. **China is not a market at all**. The Chinese consumer market isn't really a market at all. It's actually 22 distinct market clusters, each with huge variations in climate, geography, language, income levels, economies, history, and culture.

We believe that the third description is the most accurate way to define the China market, especially since consumption and hyperconsumption are no longer limited to Coastal China. Today there is consumption everywhere in China, albeit at different levels of development.

To say today that you are entering the Chinese market is akin to saying you are entering the European market. Treating China as a single, monolithic market is a recipe for disaster. It would be like entering the Netherlands, the United Kingdom, Poland, Spain, and Latvia with the same language on the packaging as well as the same product mix, pricing, merchandising, advertising, and public relations plans.

Companies must not only spend the time and resources needed to fully comprehend the nuances of common Chinese history, culture, and mind-set, but they must also spend an equal amount of time becoming familiar with China's distinct market clusters in order to understand where their products and brands best fit, where they should be launched, and where they will find their future markets. Finally, they must take care to craft brand image and marketing so as not to appear irrelevant, ignorant, or offensive in any particular cluster.

The China Whisperer

Steve Ganster is uniquely qualified and positioned to offer insight on the importance of understanding the Chinese mind-set—with its symbols, language, ethos, social complexities, and history—and how it shapes consumer behavior. There's a line in the film *Jerry Maguire* where the down-on-his-luck sports agent, Maguire, is pleading with his only client, NFL player Rod Tidwell to "Help me … help you. Help me, to help you!" In some ways, Ganster, managing director and CEO of Technomic Asia, has spent the last 25 years acting as the Jerry Maguire of China. He was one of the early movers in market-strategy consulting in China and has helped hundreds of Western firms to set up and grow their China operations over the last 30 years.

Understanding Steve's history in China and the development of Technomic Asia against China's market and consumer development is a window on the experiences of multinational firms in China. It also illuminates some of the principles for success in reaching the Chinese super consumer.

Ganster's Asian interest began at Vassar College in New York, where he received his undergraduate degree in English and Asian Studies in 1974. He says it's possible that his infatuation with Asia was triggered as a result of dating a Japanese girl while at Vassar, who inspired him to start studying the Japanese language.

After Vassar, he attended the Thunderbird School and earned a master's degree in international business. At Thunderbird, Ganster continued to study Japanese, which served him well in his early Asian forays when Japan was the focus of foreign investment in the region. In 1977, Ganster joined Technomic Consultants. Soon after joining Technomic, Ganster was asked to direct the firm's international operations. The firm already had beachheads in Europe and Latin America when Steve joined. He set up partnerships in Asia, initially in Tokyo in 1982 and then Hong Kong in 1984.

China was hardly on the radar of foreign firms at the time, given its state-run economy and closed market, not to mention its largely impoverished consumer base. Over the course of the 1980s, Japan rose but quickly started to fall from economic grace and gave way to the boom in the Southeast. Still, China was only just touching the periphery of United States and European executives' vision.

Ganster bought out the international operations of Technomic Consultants in 1986 and—with established operations in Tokyo, Singapore, and Hong Kong—he led his consulting firm into China in the mid-1980s, through a joint venture in Guangzhou with the Agriculture Industry Commerce Association (AIC), which was a portal for securing access to China-based, state-owned companies. Foreign activity in China was fairly limited at the time and there were many trade and investment barriers to participating in the local market. Given its lack of development and high risk, only a few brave companies were attempting to play in the local China market. These tended to be the leading global consumer firms like Nestlé, Procter & Gamble (P&G), Coca-Cola, and Unilever—companies already entrenched in other Asian countries and with years of experience in emerging markets.

Technomic used these pioneering years in China to build its own experience in the market, as well as to establish connections that would help them in the future. While no time line was evident, Steve was convinced that China would eventually open up to the West. This was based on signals coming from the Chinese government, which was actively exploring reform.

Ganster compares these early years of foreign entry into China to the Yukon gold rush. During these years, foreign CEOs would flock to Hong Kong, where they would make the executive cocktail circuit and tout their plans to make it big on the mainland. When these executives returned home, the task to fulfill these grandiose plans was usually left to expat management operating in a Wild West environment that lacked rule of law and a developed infrastructure.

Further, structural options to participate in the local China market were restricted primarily to joint ventures. Like the prospectors lusting for Yukon gold, though, consumer-product companies had their eye on more than 1 billion wallets. They soon found, however, that most of these were either closed or empty.

Many of the early consumer-product-based joint ventures failed for a number of reasons. The China market was still predominantly under a command-based economic system versus demand-based production. Also, Chinese consumers had little discretionary income, virtually no exposure to the West, and few places other than state-owned stores to shop.

Serving as an advisor for these early entrants, Ganster provided them with perspective on the market and their opportunities. Companies made many mistakes due to their impatience and many companies and their advisors went into the market with rose-colored glasses.

"Consumers had little to no idea what they wanted, so consumer research was largely unfruitful," Ganster says.

The lure of so many consumer wallets, ostensibly filled with cash, tempted many executives to rush through the planning process. In their minds they had a joint venture; now they simply needed the structure to start selling. In addition, in these early days, China's consumer boom had not started and the dream of Chinese super consumers was a long way off.

Spinning in a Whirlpool

One early example of this leap-of-faith approach was Whirlpool, the venerable American white goods company. Whirlpool paid a high tuition cost to enter China, as Mark Hu, Whirlpool's previous Asia vice president, puts it: "Prior to the major opening of China in the 1990s, the three big buys for Chinese consumers were bicycles, watches, and sewing machines. In the 1990s, this shifted to televisions, washing machines, and refrigerators. When Whirlpool came calling in the early 1990s, the appliance market was booming. So was corporate optimism and perhaps naiveté."

In September 1995, management announced the company's fifth China joint-venture agreement in less than a year, with total investments of more than $100 million. Management created Whirlpool's T-4 strategy for China, attacking the top four major domestic appliance categories all at once: refrigerators, washing machines, microwave ovens, and air conditioners. Comments from Whirlpool executives, which echoed the statements of many other foreign firms at the time, often included phrases like, "We look forward to a long and successful partnership, building on each other's significant strengths."

Whirlpool's so-called honeymoon lasted just three years with these partners. In 1998, it pulled out of a Shenzhen air-conditioning venture and also exited the refrigerator joint venture it had formed with

Beijing Snowflake. As Whirlpool management has admitted, it bought into the China craze without a clearly defined China strategy or understanding of history and culture, and quickly jumped into joint ventures without insight into Chinese consumer needs and purchase motivators. The company fed these consumer products that did not meet their needs and weren't competitive with upstart Chinese appliance makers, such as Haier. For many companies, like Whirlpool, it was a foregone conclusion that they "had to be in China." And many of these other firms suffered a similar fate.

The Great Pizza Wars: In China, Everything Is Possible, but Nothing Is Easy

Ganster recalls that, in these early years, he preached "Observe the 6 Ds: due diligence, due diligence, due diligence." The Chinese government often served up potential partners to foreign firms and management did not do its homework on them. The government's blessing seemed enough assurance that all would be well. Of course, this was not the case.

A good contrast in company approaches is well represented by what we call "The Great Pizza Wars." Domino's and Pizza Hut took very different approaches to the China market, with very different results. Pizza Hut analyzed the market, studied Chinese attitudes and understanding of foreign foods and restaurants, dining habits, food preferences, and ultimately how best to "China-fy" its value proposition. As a result, it has been China's largest and most successful foreign casual dining chain in China with more than 1,300 restaurants, and it's still growing. But is it casual dining? For many middle-class consumers, a meal at Pizza Hut in China is still akin to fine dining. The menu features dozens of items ranging from pasta and pizza to Chinese spicy hot wings. Diners relax in well appointed, spotless restaurants, get a level of service rare in China, and are proud to take dates, colleagues, and family there for a long, Chinese style meal. Chinese diners especially love eating their personal size pizzas with a knife and fork, making for an authentic Western experience.

Domino's, however, did not observe the 6 Ds and charged ahead with its established business model … and failed miserably. The lack of due diligence led the company to assume it could, and promised consumers it would, deliver within 30 minutes, in what is often gridlock traffic conditions on most Chinese city centers. It offered only take-out service, which was not culturally accepted. It did not account for the family dynamic (When a large pizza was delivered to an apartment complex, relatives and friends would descend on the unsuspecting diners to get their share of the pie!). Its flavors were not adapted to local tastes, nor was the size of the pizza, which was too large and cumbersome to eat while walking down the street, never mind the refinement of eating with fork and knife. Plus, no restaurants. Today, Domino's has fewer than 40 restaurants in China and is basically irrelevant. Due diligence is still just as important. Though much has improved in terms of information access, the market and its players tend to remain relatively opaque (as typified by the common occurrence of multiple sets of financial books). You have to search hard to find what you need in order to validate your strategy in China—and, even then, the level of uncertainty will be higher than it would be for an investment in a developed country.

Listen to the Great One

The pace of change in China, though slowed from the 1990s and 2000s, is still rapid today compared to the West. By the time you figure out the market, it's changed. As hockey great Wayne Gretzky used to say, "Skate where the puck is going, not where it's been."

Procter & Gamble exemplifies this forward thinking in China through its Two-Dollar-a-Day project. While its core business in China focuses on the more affluent consumer, who will spend $10 for a bottle of shampoo, management is looking ahead to the super consumers who reside deep in the countryside. These consumers typically earn less than $2,000 a year but they also have needs and desires when it comes to beauty and hygiene. P&G has devoted a significant amount of research to understanding the emerging super consumer's wants and limitations in order to design products and price points that would sell. As a result, it is creating brand awareness and loyalty. P&G is a great case study of an early entrant who had experienced great success in China, reading the tea leaves on the transition from consumer boom to super consumption. They offer something for almost every level of consumer in China. China's consumers have boosted their bottom line and provided a still fast growing market for its products to offset slowdowns in other markets.

Ganster says that a lesson learned that applies to virtually all of consumer companies today is the importance of understanding your addressable market(s), where you can make money and where your value proposition plays well. With more than 1.3 billion consumers with vastly different profiles (versus the initial years under the command economy), identifying addressable markets is critical.

"Most markets in China are big and growing but that does not mean your product or service fits well at an acceptable price point (with acceptable margin)," he says. "You need to understand the main market segments, their needs and wallet size, and then design an appropriate strategy and business model to penetrate them. It is rare that a company can simply transplant its business model to China."

Ganster uses the expression China-fy in this regard, and World Kitchen (Corelle, Pyrex, and CorningWare brands) presents an interesting example of China-fying. In the United States, World Kitchen sells predominantly through mass-market channels to middle-income consumers. A dinner plate sells for between three and four dollars. Not fine china, for sure. However, in China, its consumer profile is very different. Middle-income consumers are not the target and mass-market channels are not the main outlet for its products. In China, Corelle is high end, and it sells through department stores like Mitsukoshi, Parkson, and Sogo.

World Kitchen management found its addressable market with these higher-income consumers who shop at upmarket retail establishments. While initially developing this core addressable market, management is cultivating the evolving middle-class consumers—and more mass-market channels—as they both rapidly develop.

Stay the Course, Even When the Seas Get Rough

A solid and long-term commitment to Chinese consumers will provide stability when the inevitable storms roll in. Not long after companies enter China market, the luster can dull on the pot of gold, which management was counting on. In Steve's words, it turned into fool's gold. Without a strong and undaunting commitment from company stakeholders, it will be difficult to hold the course through these storms.

We can compare China's consumer market evolution to the nature of human development, which provides an interesting and helpful way to understand the context of the market landscape that you are dealing in, as well as the consumers themselves.

In the early, toddler phase of China's development the market was in its formative stages, just starting to crawl and walk. Rambunctious, mobile, and caught in a riptide of emotion, toddlers are uncultivated, pedal-to-the-metal humans. China's market personality was showing signs of its main traits but we still had little idea of what China would look like as an adult. You can imagine how difficult it was to develop a sound market strategy then.

As the market grew and moved into its adolescent years, the challenges in many ways became greater. Teens often change their interests, clothing styles, and general identities on a fairly regular basis. This is because they are exploring themselves as individuals. So, too, did the China market convey similar turbulence as the government, market forces, and consumers struggled to adjust to the market's growing pains. Multinational companies have to deal with similar issues as parents do with teenagers during this period—mood swings, desire for privacy, risk taking, and rebelliousness.

If we monitor China's consumers over this development period, we see tremendous change. In the 1990s, during the toddler years, China's consumers were figuratively spoon-fed. Disposable income was a paltry $500 to $600 a year in the mid-1990s, and the concept of consumer credit was basically unheard of. It was a seller's market. Consumers followed trends blindly with little access to information, as China was still quite closed to the Western media. For instance, the red dress prevailed in the 1990s and every woman at that time was eager to have one in order to be a trendsetter.

As China moved into its teen years in the 2000s, there was much more product availability and choice, which started to convert the market into one for buyers. Consumers were becoming more sophisticated. They started to compare price, quality, and service. Nowadays, consumers pursue uniqueness and a tailor-made approach. They don't want the same red dress anymore. Instead, they prefer dresses that show their individuality. They also care more about product quality and safety.

With the increase in disposable income, which reached levels closer to $1,500 by 2005, consumers became segmented into layers—upper class, middle class, and mass. Brands and products started to cater to these specific segments. With disposable income increasing by 4×, 5×,

8×, and 10× since then and with new consumers coming online, there are five to six layers that companies must strategize for and around.

Nestlé: Navigating the Teen Years

Nestlé followed two key principles in its strategy: It took a long-term view and patiently built a presence that matched the evolutionary phases of the Chinese consumer. Its goal has been to win the war, not the battle. Nestlé was an early mover in China, having opened its first sales office in Shanghai in 1908. In 1990, seeing the door opening wider to the market, the company ramped up its activity and started local production by establishing its first factory in Shuangcheng, Heilongjiang Province.

It adopted an effective approach through this formula:

Local insights + Nestlé technology = winning recipe.

Nestlé effectively China-fied its offering by adapting product tastes and formats to local preferences. Today, Nestlé has nearly 50,000 employees, 15 partnerships, more than 30 factories, and two research and development centers in China. They have a multitude of products on the shelves of a diverse set of channels and have become in many ways a "Chinese" brand. Their constant innovation, long-term investment, and patience have positioned them to be a leader in China for a long time to come. Perhaps just as importantly though, Chinese consumers have told Nestlé what they want and the company has created products just for them, producing billions of dollars in revenue that would otherwise not exist. This has had the knock-on effect of allowing Nestlé to be more innovative and aggressive in other markets, becoming the largest food and beverage company in the world.

China is now a young adult, certainly more mature but still subject to directional shifts. And like a young adult, the Chinese consumer is spreading his or her wings, even flying to cities all over the world. With disposable income at more than 50 times what is was before China opened its markets, the Chinese super consumer has the money, the sophistication, and the access to buy anything they want, almost anywhere they want. It will be interesting, as well as strategically critical, to closely follow these super consumers as they move into full adulthood and middle age.

Over the last three decades, business-growth strategy has evolved in tune with China's maturation and the development of the super consumer. It has moved from the tendency for designing crude strategies simply to be in the market to creating sophisticated and precise strategies that target multiple consumer groups with specific value propositions.

"We preach the mantra of strategy before structure with all of our clients," Steve Ganster says, "One thing that separates the winners from the losers in China is that the winners spend more time and resources on research that leads to smart decisions on ideal market, operations, product type, launch, and growth strategies, with an early focus on culture and history."

This may sound somewhat obvious, but many companies focus on quickly building a structure with a see-what-sticks approach to strategy. After understanding that China is made up of many markets within a larger market, we can broadly define the China market as the place where companies, after establishing solid entry strategies, establish their operations.

It is where their legal entity, usually in the form of a WOFE (wholly foreign-owned enterprise), FICE (foreign-invested corporate entity), or joint venture is based. It is where they will establish an office, hire employees, and pay taxes. It is where they make, import, ship, store, distribute, and sell their products through numerous sales channels.

It is where companies advertise in magazines, on radio, on TV, and online; where they deploy public relations strategies; and where they hope Chinese consumers will engage with them directly. It is where they hope to sell physical products to Chinese consumers face-to-face or online.

But China's super consumers have created an entirely new demographic, an entirely new market, and a need for companies to engage them globally, not just within a set of borders.

CHAPTER 13

The China Global Demographic

As Chinese consumers have become not just more sophisticated, but in many cases super sophisticated and after 20 years of buying virtually everything available inside the China market, a new demographic has emerged—a demographic that has helped define and expand the reach and impact of the world's second coming of the super consumer: We call it the China Global Demographic Market (CGDM).

More and more Chinese have started to travel the world for business, pleasure, and study (much as their American predecessors did). In fact, some 200,000 Chinese students per year are enrolled at American universities and another 100,000 per year are studying in Europe. China's going-global phenomenon has exploded. These students have changed the fortunes of many universities by paying full tuition and adding a richness and diversity to the student body, and many colleges and universities have set up recruiting offices in China to attract these students.

They are from Shanghai and Beijing, from Chengdu and Chongqing, from Taishan and Taiwan. They are from every city and market cluster. They are influenced by what they see, hear, taste, and experience abroad. They are the consumers who took Club Med in Maldives from a 5 percent Chinese customer base to 80 percent in the last five years. Chinese super consumers are a new global demographic. Twenty-five percent of all luxury purchases globally are made by Chinese consumers, and 60 percent of those transactions take place outside Mainland China.

Brands, retailers, service providers, and any company hoping to engage Chinese consumers must adapt to a new reality: Focusing on the China market(s) is no longer enough to succeed. In some cases, marketing and selling your products exclusively within the borders of China is a recipe for abject failure.

To be sure, the emergence of the CGDM does not substantially decrease the importance of the mainland regarding sales, marketing, branding, and sales success, especially for mass and mid-market products and brands. But for premium and luxury products or brands, companies must understand, integrate, and live in both the mainland and international markets.

The Precious Gift of Time

For a better sense of the ways that successful premium and luxury brands and retailers are reshaping their strategies to maximize their ability to serve the global Chinese super consumer, let's take Tourneau, the world's largest watch retailer.

It was a frigid February 2014 evening and there were not too many people walking outside. However, inside the elegant four-story flagship store, Ira Melnitsky, CEO of luxury watch retailer Tourneau, was speaking almost-perfect Mandarin to nearly 800 Chinese consumers, wishing them "Happy Chinese New Year." As he ended his remarks, a group of musicians with gongs, taiko drums, and cymbals started to perform the Chinese lion dance with one gold and one red lion. Melnitsky and the other VIP cohosts were feeding the lions cabbage placed at the end of a fishing pole, thus ensuring good luck.

The atmosphere was cheerful. Hundreds of Chinese consumers wished each other New Year's greetings in Mandarin, Cantonese, or Shanghai-ese while admiring the latest timepieces from Rolex, Patek Philippe, Cartier, Longines, and others, in the store. This scene did not take place in Hong Kong or China, but rather in New York City—not in Chinatown either, but in the heart of midtown Manhattan on Madison Avenue and 57th Street, next to the flagship store of Nike and across the street from Chanel and Christian Dior.

When the event ended, the guests received a parting gift bag from Tourneau, including a copy of its annual catalog, a Year of the Horse commemorative coin, and a special-edition box of Year of the Horse chocolates from Godiva.

To capture the Chinese Global Consumer, Tourneau's management team understands that they are both truly global and highly mobile, especially when the Chinese tax on luxury watches can be higher than 50 percent. The huge price gap between luxury goods sold in China and abroad has also led to massive luxury consumption outflows. High import duties and consumption taxes levied on luxury watches have pushed up the prices in China. For example, the consumption tax on luxury watches in China is 20 percent and the import tariff is somewhere between 11 and 100 percent. As a result, the median price of a Cartier tank watch is $4,409 in the United States versus $5,996 in China, a 36 percent difference in price. According to the research done by World Luxury Association, during the Chinese New Year in 2013, Chinese consumers spent as much as $8.5 billion on luxury goods abroad, up by 18 percent compared to the year before. Chinese consumers spent the most on luxury watches, followed by leather goods, apparel, cosmetics, and perfume.

Chinese luxury consumers, especially many government officials and private entrepreneurs, love to show off their timepieces. We vividly remembered one of our meetings in Beijing with six successful chairmen of private companies. Each wore a different model of Patek Philippe, and they spent half the meeting talking about their timepieces, including the unique features and where they purchased them.

According to a report by KPMG, 72 percent of traveling Chinese consumers purchased luxury items during their overseas trips. This data bodes well for Tourneau. Founded in 1900, Tourneau has over 30 stores throughout North America. It has invested a great deal to nurture and capture both Chinese tourists and domestic Chinese consumers. Tourneau understands the motivation of the Chinese customer, who comes to buy luxury brand watches, such as Vacheron Constantin, Jaeger LeCoultre, and Blancpain, and also luxury-lite brands, such as TAG Heuer, Hamilton, and Tissot. Tourneau hits both luxury and high-end consumer markets and, at the same time, is learning about the culture and behavior of Chinese consumers by sending staff to China every year to meet with various travel agencies and government officials in order to fine tune their marketing strategies and adjust their projections.

Melnitsky says that "the nature of our store locations in major cities like New York, Los Angeles, and Hawaii, and even Miami, have always been in glamorous locations to serve the local customers and to attract the tourists to shop. Like the Japanese tourists in the 1980s, Chinese tourists have become a very important group of customers for the last five years and we've learned to serve them culturally and appropriately."

Some Chinese tourists like to shop in groups, according to Melnitsky, and Tourneau is hiring more Mandarin-speaking personnel to handle them.

"One thing that seems to be quite consistent is that the appreciation of luxury goods carries pretty evenly among different cultures," Melnitsky says. "For the Chinese tourists and local customers, the appreciation for better goods is very consistent. It is our job to learn more about the culture, their preference of credit cards, and the important concept of gifting.

"Our sales professionals tell us that the Chinese shopping transactions sometimes take a different path—meaning they want to continue shopping, and sharing of product information, sometimes digitally by taking a picture and sharing through WeChat. Our vice president of marketing, Richard Gellman, and our director of marketing, Melanie Rudin, are becoming experts in learning about Chinese culture and travel and it has benefitted Tourneau immensely."

Before joining Tourneau, Melnitsky was a senior executive at Li & Fung, the huge Hong Kong-based global sourcing company. He traveled extensively in China, which helped prepare him for his current role at Tourneau. His understanding of Chinese culture is vastly superior to a traditional local business executive who hasn't traveled to China or Asia, and he says that educating his team on the Chinese mind-set and cultural nuances is critical. In fact, he has sent Gellman and Rudin to China specifically to meet with local watch retailers and to learn what they sell so Tourneau can remain at the forefront of any changes in taste and styles.

"It is an education process," Melnitsky says. "Our executives go every year because Chinese consumers are evolving and getting more sophisticated. Gellman and Rudin come back and write up their findings and share them with the entire organization. Those learnings come into play, and we put them into our store training. As we bring more native Chinese-speaking people into our employment, they also help us evolve to be more culturally appropriate and effective."

In recent years, however, China's economy has slowed from a super-sonic sprint to a steadily paced run. At the same time, China's president Xi Jinping has started to crack down on spending by officials. Luxury has, for officials at least, become a new minefield to negotiate. Internet users are on the lookout for Chinese government officials who display signs of ill-gotten gains. The former head of Shaanxi Province's Bureau of Work Safety was sentenced to 14 years in prison after being convicted of corruption, a charge brought about after a Chinese *netizen* circulated multiple images of him wearing more than 10 different luxury time-pieces, including a Vacheron Constantin worth more than $33,000. This earned him the nickname Brother Watch.

Without question, certain sectors have been hit hard by the anti-graft crusade, especially those most associated with gift giving, such as premium spirits and watch brands. Nevertheless, Tourneau has yet to feel the effects of a slowing economy and government anticorruption efforts.

"I haven't seen any decrease in our store traffic yet, maybe because of our efforts in targeting second- and third-tier tourists from China and the percentage of those customers are growing at a healthy pace," Melnitsky says.

Even if the anticorruption drive will slow down business gift-gifting, thereby weakening the demand for luxury goods, some people believe that this would only be a temporary phenomenon, as gift giving is deeply rooted in Chinese culture. In fact, a large majority of gift giving is for legitimate personal gifting among friends.

The luxury gift of time is still one of the best gifts in the world. Melnitsky recalls that—long after the Chinese consumers finished their transactions at the New Year's event—they stayed to enjoy their Chinese teas and continue browsing at the latest watches. Their appetite to learn about new products is voracious and shopping is still a novel experience. Well-trained staff know not to rush the Chinese super consumer.

Meet the Tangs

Perhaps the easiest way to explain the China global demographic is to join a family, one at the more sophisticated end of the consumer scale, on a typical January trip abroad. This family, the Tangs, are a composite of dozens we know, and everything in their story is accurate and true for hundreds of thousands of Chinese. Their new habits, desires and dreams, self-image, real and perceived needs, and spending patterns illustrate why many companies need to serve the China market and the China global demographic.

The Tang family: Mr. Tang, 46; Mrs. Tang, 44; Bo "Bobby" Tang, 16; and Mr. Tang's parents, Tang Wei, 67, and Tang Lao Shi, 68.

Mr. Tang is a wealthy businessman from Suzhou, a booming and beautiful city in Jiangsu Province and a satellite of Shanghai. He opened a home decoration manufacturing company in 1998. His business grew rapidly as he made products for American and European brands, which he sold, through importers, to big retailers like Macy's; Target; Bed, Bath and Beyond; Carrefour; and Tesco.

Within five years, he had enough money to invest in other businesses, including partial ownership in other housewares manufacturing companies. By 2007, he also owned five car dealerships in Suzhou, had a partial interest in a local brewery, and was one of three partners in a chain of local restaurants.

His family became accustomed to dining in the best restaurants, spending heavily on luxury cars, fashion, accessories, and *badge brands* that identified them as part of China's nouveau riche. They also began traveling frequently to Macao for gambling, Hong Kong for shopping, and Thailand for beach holidays.

Mr. Tang acquired foreign credit cards—as well as his China Union Pay Card—and became an elite member of the Marriott Rewards Club and United Premier. It was around this time that the Tang family invested heavily in Shanghai real estate and made its first apartment purchase in the United States. In 2012, Mr. Tang became an early investor in a Beijing mobile app and gaming startup that went public 18 months later. Meanwhile, he had tripled his number of car dealerships to 15.

Mrs. Tang is the only daughter of a Tianjin family that runs a knitting factory founded in the early 1970s. Originally, the factory was state owned (her father was the manager) and made socks, gloves, and caps for the People's Liberation Army. In 1995, during the first wave of massive privatization, her father was allowed to buy the company from the state and take it private. Soon, it was making more than 30 million pairs of socks and gloves for export each year. She was educated at a good university in China, and spent a year studying at Northeastern University in Boston. After graduation, she worked for a time in the family business, and her contacts with foreign clients and experience in international trade led to a job with a foreign consulting firm in Shanghai.

Tang Bo was born in 1998. He was destined to be an only child, like all of his peers, because of China's one-child policy, in place since the early 1980s (in 2014 the policy was largely rescinded). Like the generation born before him in the 1980s and early 1990s, the only China he knows is the New China—a rising China, a wealthier China, a China where opportunities abound for talented and hard-working young people, a China where Bo could build on the success of his parents or strike out on his own.

Bo was born into the China that was also giving birth to the China dream and the Chinese super consumer. He and his demographic brothers and sisters were soon called little emperors and little princesses because their success and happiness were the sole focus of their parents and grandparents. They were doted on and pampered. Bo went to a premier private high school and was given the best things in life.

The family first flies to Seattle to visit Mr. Tang's sister and her family (his brother-in-law shuttles between Seattle and Beijing for his business and another in which he coinvested with Mr. Tang). They eat, drink, and reconnect. They also discuss how their cousins in Toronto are doing. From Seattle, they fly to Los Angeles and spend two days at Disneyland, where a luxury concierge service set them up with VIP passes and a guide. They then spent three days at a luxury hotel, where celebrities have lived and played for decades. This is an experiential luxury that makes them feel good and will provide great *face* when they go home. They shop on Rodeo Drive and a couple of well-known malls, and they also spend a day at a movie studio.

From L.A., they fly to Boston, where they will spend the next three days. They visit Harvard, MIT, Boston College, and Tufts for Bo; visit Quincy Market for a real American experience; and they meet with realtors to find an apartment for Bo—and one for the family—if he chooses to go to college in Boston. They finish with a whale-watching trip.

From Boston, they fly to New York City, where they visit Columbia and NYU and also meet with the realtor who helped Mr. Tang purchase a $3 million dollar apartment on the Upper East Side two years prior. They spend their days shopping on Madison and Fifth Avenues. At night, they eat in the best restaurants (from a list one of Mr. Tang's Fudan University classmates, now working on Wall Street, made for him). Mrs. Tang buys some jewelry at Tiffany's.

They leave New York after four days and fly to Las Vegas for three more days. To fulfill their desire for more experiential luxury, they take a private helicopter tour of the Grand Canyon; they go to a shooting club and fire off .50 caliber machine guns; and they drink at exclusive nightclubs.

During the course of the trip the Tangs have engaged in the activities and absorbed the experiences that typify the characteristics, desires, and spending habits of the Chinese global demographic.

- A well-off Chinese family with a father engaged in international business.
- Family living in North America and/or Europe.
- Widespread connections in the Chinese diaspora.
- Engagement with airlines, hotels, specialty concierge companies, and a plethora of other service providers.
- Engagement with known brands and retailers while discovering new ones.
- Preparation for their child to be educated in the United States or Europe.
- Looking to add to their US real estate holdings.
- A new understanding that doesn't just include buying luxury items but experiencing a luxury lifestyle.
- Go home with great memories and more consumer sophistication, as well as a desire to engage brands at home, use social media to tell their stories, and make plans for the next trip.

The Tangs have made the most of the New China. Through hard work, intelligence, and the right connections, they were part of the first wave of newly wealthy consumers who helped fuel the initial consumer boom of the 2000s. As they got wealthier, traveled more, and as more families like theirs came to the fore, they helped launch the Chinese super consumer era. Now, they are at the forefront of taking this phenomenon global.

"The Chinese government expects to issue 200 million new passports in the next ten years," says Christine Lu, cofounder and CEO of Affinity China, a company focused on Chinese global travelers seeking exclusive experiences. "There are already about 80–90 million Chinese passports. China going global has and will continue to disrupt the hospitality industry, global retail, banking, real estate, education, and the service sectors. Global Chinese consumers will help make or break companies and industries in the next 5–10 years."

CHAPTER 14

Channels

The number and type of sales channels that became legal and then proliferated, from roughly 2000 to 2010, were a key growth driver of the Chinese consumer boom. As we have seen, an early impediment to the growth of consumer culture was that it was at first limited to a number of state-owned shops. This was followed by a period where joint ventures provided a model, but a risky and less than ideal one, to sell products.

There were two keys to the creation and proliferation of channels, which gave birth to hyperconsumption leading into the 2000s:

1. Government rules, regulations, and laws opening the way for relatively easy entry and establishment of retail entities and entry into existing sales channels by foreign companies.
2. The already-in-place foundation of traditional Chinese retail and sales channels that could be engaged with, built upon, and partnered with.

Today, China is the top market in the world for new retail space construction, accounting for more than half of global shopping center development.

It is important for brands and retailers to understand all of the distribution channels available to them in China and to understand the pros and cons of each. There are traditional distribution channels and new channels. Retail sales in some of the new channels are experiencing rapid growth.

"With the unprecedented pace of urbanization and a rising middle class, there is an increasing demand for modern shopping facilities in China," says Frank Chen, executive director and head of CBRE Research China, a commercial and real estate services firm.

We will start by defining the traditional channels of retail in China and then do the same for China's modern and newly developed channels. By understanding each, you'll be able to determine how, when, and why brands and products should or should not be sold in each. Also, note that we'll dig into e-commerce in Chapter 15.

Department Stores

Department stores were among the first Western-style retail environments to take root in China.

Not surprisingly though, proto-department stores, like many other Western ideas, were originally founded and developed in China, as far back as 1,000 years ago. They became fixed and permanent alternatives to monthly or weekly markets, traveling farmers, and peddlers. These multidepartment structures were often two, three, or even four stories high; floors and sections were divided for selling food items, Chinese medicine, clothing, tools, and household products. From a combination of Chinese history, tradition, and early-Western influence, department stores were and are very much a part of Chinese culture and consumption. But, there are huge differences between Chinese department stores and Western-style department stores.

In the West, a department store offers a multitude of brands in departments. There is a corporate headquarters staff by the C-level executives, mid-level executives, accountants, lawyers, buyers, merchandisers, advertising and public relations staff, front and back-office personnel, an e-commerce team, forecasting and replenishment experts, and logistics and supply chain professionals. The network of stores follows the strategic and practical decisions made at corporate, and there is a uniformity of the stores regarding layout, merchandising, decoration, advertising and categories, brands, and styles carried.

In China, department store business models are different. There are big corporations, like Parkson, New World, and Orient, who have multiple stores across China. As in the West, there are national, regional, provincial, and municipal chains. There are also a great many department stores that are single entities or have only two or three locations.

The major difference between Western and Chinese department stores is that Chinese department stores, unlike their Western counterparts, are *not merchants who hold inventory and practice merchandising; they are landlords who rent out space to brands.* This has and likely will continue to baffle and challenge some brands. The realization that the brand must in essence become a retailer is a hard model for many to accept.

Department stores in China usually have several floors, each floor containing several categories. Cosmetics and body care on the first floor; women's wear on the second; men's wear on the third; baby products, children's wear, and toys on the fourth. But the floor space is akin to the mall model. Brands rent or lease a space on a floor. They can then design a store on the floor or can build-out a mini-store along the edges on the floor. Brands pay the monthly rent as well as a percentage of sales to the storeowner. The only way to deliver product to stores is through national, regional, and local distributors.

There are no corporate buyers in China. Brands do not operate on the wholesale/retail model that dominates in the West. The property owners have the power to decide who and who not to allow in the department store, but once a lease is signed it is up to the brand to determine its own product mix, deliver product, hire sales staff, merchandise, and become de facto retailers.

In addition to high import tariffs, payments to distributors, rental costs for floor space, and the practice of owing a percentage of sales to the property owner are some of the reasons why products in China cost anywhere from 30 to 50 percent more than in other parts of the world.

Street-Level Stores

Street-level stores have an even longer history in China than department stores. Traders and purveyors of everything Chinese urban dwellers needed sold merchandise in street-level stores of myriad sizes and varieties throughout Chinese history. Today's stand-alone, street-level stores are a continuation of this long tradition, with the difference being the number of foreign-owned stores.

As with department stores, however, there are some key differences between Western and Chinese stand-alone stores. The most glaring difference is that the vast majority modern of Chinese stores, as well as foreign-owned, street-level ones are single brand. If you were to stroll down Hua Hai Zhong Lu, Shanghai's Fifth Avenue, you would find the huge flagship stores of Coach, H&M, Uniqlo, Zara, Zegna, Sephora, and Lane Crawford.

If you continued strolling you would find the smaller stores for Rolex, Hublot, Harry Winston, Shanghai Tang, Li Ning, and China's (as well as the world's) largest jewelry retailer, Chow Tai Fook.

There are a number of stores in certain categories that are multi-brand. One example is the Shanghai #1 Bedding store, on Nanjing Xi Lu, where you can find local and foreign bedroom textile and mattress brands. Another is Kate Zhou Handbags. Zhou has stores in Shanghai, Beijing, and Guangzhou, and she sells niche luxury brands like Tusk, Rebecca Minkoff, and Magnes Sisters.

But multibrand retailing in street-level stores is still in its infancy in China. Stand-alone stores in China can be expensive to set up due to high rents and high build-out costs. Another challenge is finding and securing good locations. This is an issue with mall stores as well. We find that it's wise to engage retail real estate experts for this.

There are many advantages to street-level stores in China, although their importance in the most developed cities seems to be contracting a bit as cost goes up, returns are harder to earn, and e-commerce becomes more important.

That said, street-level stores allow brands to better express themselves through merchandising and build credibility with wary Chinese consumers. There are a number of disadvantages as well. Expansion and scaling is complicated and expensive. Finding the balance between incremental, learning-based growth, and meeting increased market demand requires a great deal of study.

Despite the challenges that come with operating street-level stores, most companies and brands still need at least one flagship store and a number of satellite stores. Chinese consumers respond to the brand awareness and credibility that stores provide. They want to spend time in the store, poring over and touching products. At the luxury level, these stores provide for an environment where special services can be rendered for wealthy customers—private shopping hours, secret rooms, and exclusive merchandise, for example.

Malls

The first Western-style malls started to appear in Beijing in the years from 1987 to 1991. Many were invested in and built by Hong Kong and Taiwan-based developers who had years of experience operating malls in those markets, as well as in other places in Asia. After Deng's Southern Tour, which among other things declared that Shanghai be encouraged to absorb foreign investment, more mall developers came into Shanghai. From 1995 onward, malls started to spread out from Shanghai and Beijing to other first- and second-tier cities in northern, eastern, and southern China.

In those days, and even into the 2000s, many mall stores were money losers for brands and retailers. Rents were high and, while foot traffic was robust, very few shoppers spent money. Chinese shoppers used the malls for afternoon outings and places to socialize or find respite from extreme heat or cold. But they also got an education in modern retail and exposure to new brands, and they found out what was popular in the outside world.

At first, retailers and brands accepted that they would have to endure money-losing operations in the short term on their way to long-term success. This included their presence in malls as well as street-level stores and department stores. Those that were willing and able to stick it out eventually started to see healthy returns.

Unlike department stores, the malls in China operate in a similar fashion to the Western model. A developer or owner operates the mall, store space is rented from the owners, while brands and retailers build out and operate their store. They are free to operate and present themselves as they wish, as long as they comply with the mall's common standards. One aspect that is different—although this is changing, as overcapacity becomes a problem—is that the mall owner reserves the right to terminate a store's lease if it's not performing well.

There are different levels of malls, from mid-market, to premium, to luxury. There are also specialty malls that focus on certain demographics. However, malls in China differ from their Western counterparts in a number of ways. These include:

- Where most malls in the United States are single- or two-story affairs, Chinese malls typically have four to six levels.
- Rents are highest on the first floor and cheapest on the top floor.
- Foot traffic decreases significantly with each floor.
- Chinese malls usually feature a wide array of dining choices concentrated on a single floor. These can range from snack stands, to mid-price restaurants, to expensive and well-known restaurants.

- A store may be removed from the mall for nonperformance.
- Many malls have a basement floor that also features restaurants, but also large, modern, high-end grocery stores.

Some malls in China also now feature husband daycares. Known in Chinese as "laogong jicun chu" (老公寄存处), which literally translates to "husband cloakroom," these rooms provide men with a place to relax, lounge, read the paper, check their phones, and do anything but shop.

By 2010, malls were ubiquitous in almost every developed Chinese city. In fact, by 2014, there were maybe too many malls in China, an estimated 3,000 and, according to CBRE Research China, there will be more than 4,000 by 2016. Overcapacity and underuse in the last few years have become common, and they are worth tracking for brands and retailers alike.

The role that malls play for you, and the ways in which Chinese consumers shop at malls, is changing. Harking back to the similarities between the American Dream and the Chinese Dream, maturity in China's consumer market means that consumers are spending more money at malls. Like in the United States during the 1970s and 1980s, malls have become centers of youth culture, places for teens to hang out and socialize, where they can shape and act out who they are. Malls also provide senior citizens with a place to walk, talk, and socialize.

Apparel, footwear, and accessories still perform very well in malls, but mall stores are not meant for every category or brand. You must measure this channel against others before choosing malls as part of your retail strategy. We have seen many a bedding, electronics, and home décor retailer die on the sixth floor.

Grocery Stores/Supermarkets

In 2012, China overtook the United States as the largest grocery market in the world. According to IGD, a food and beverage industry research and consulting company, the Chinese grocery market was worth $1 trillion in 2013, and IGD expects the market to be worth $1.5 trillion by 2016.

These numbers are an astounding example of the emergence of China's super consumers. Remember, this was a country that just 30 years ago issued food-ration cards. Little more than 20 years ago, the

Chinese consumer spent the vast majority of his or her food money buying daily needs at fresh meat and produce markets.

Large, Western-style grocery stores emerged as a channel in the mid-2000s when many malls, luxury apartment buildings, and office towers started to feature them in their lower levels. In the early years, they were concentrated heavily in the top 10 markets, where they catered mostly to foreign expatriates, the wealthy, and curious emerging middle-class consumers.

Over the past 10 years, supermarkets have become an increasingly more important channel for fast-moving consumer goods, such as health, beauty, and body-care products, and Western food and beverage companies. Many rival their counterparts in the United States in terms of size, type, and number of products for sale, and merchandising sophistication. For instance, children's cereal can be found on the lowest shelves in China.

Modern Chinese grocery stores often feature prepared-food sections, extensive wine, beer, and liquor sections, and a wide array of local and imported foods. While grocery stores are becoming ever more important as a channel, they still have a relatively low penetration and market share in China. But as urbanization continues, and more people enter the middle class, the potential for continued growth is high. If development patterns continue it is quite possible that grocery stores will be as ubiquitous in China as they are in the West.

Hypermarkets

Hypermarkets, or supercenters, are combinations of grocery stores and department stores, and now often have pharmacies and service centers within the stores. In the West, early hypermarket innovators included Fred Myer, a chain based in the American Pacific Northwest, and Carrefour, which was founded in France in 1963.

From these early beginnings evolved Walmart, Kmart, and Target, which introduced hypermarkets, superstores, and wholesale clubs. They typically feature huge footprints—120,000 to 250,000 square feet—and rely on high-volume, low-margin business models. In the United States, hypermarkets are beginning to lose their luster as the combination of e-commerce, reurbanization, and specialty retailers take market share away from them. But, like malls and department stores, a model that is fading somewhat in the United States and Europe has found new and vibrant life in China.

As in the West, hypermarkets are usually located outside city centers where they provide one-stop shopping for nearby residents, who will typically shop there, on average, once a week. They also feature very large footprints, typically 100,000 square feet, and large product selections, often more than 20,000 items. Hypermarkets, foreign-owned and domestic, also tend to buy most goods directly from factories. This is an advantage because of China's importance as a consumer-product producer. It is also an advantage when sourcing local food and beverage items. It does, however, present logistical and cost challenges when it comes to foreign-sourced goods. They usually overcome this issue by purchasing through distributors, who also provide them with stocking and warehousing help.

Hypermarkets present foreign and local brands an opportunity for large-volume sales, but as with hypermarkets in the West, margins are tight.

Chinese consumers are spending more time and more money at hypermarkets. This is especially true of Chinese families, who live in the outer suburbs and who are modeling their lifestyle on the American suburban way of life. It is notable that, with the lifting of the one-child policy, hypermarkets may become an even more important channel for producers and consumers alike in the future.

According to PricewaterhouseCoopers (PwC), China will overtake the United States as the world's largest retail market by 2016 with $4.2 trillion in sales, and hypermarkets should lead the way. Still, there are many challenges ahead for the continued growth of hypermarkets in China. After nine years in China operating as an independent entity, British hypermarket Tesco is folding its operations into a joint venture with the state-run supermarket operator China Resources Enterprise.

Convenience Stores

7-Eleven, the largest, most well-known chain of convenience stores in the United States, is not only a large and important sales channel for thousands of companies—and a daily part of the lives of millions of Americans—but it and its competitors in the convenience-store market have become ubiquitous icons of American consumption.

Convenience stores have become an important modern sales channel in China as well. 7-Eleven opened its first store in Guangdong Province in China in 1992. It followed the path of incremental growth, taking care to learn from the market over the long term as an investment for the future. It did not expand to Beijing until 2004, followed by openings in Chengdu and Shanghai in 2011, Qingdao in 2012, and Chongqing in 2013.

The vast majority of the stock carried is food and beverage, but a significant inventory of health, beauty, and body-care products are on offer as well.

Family Mart, a Japanese-operated company, entered China around the same time as 7-Eleven and has grown exponentially as well. Other players in the market are Lawson and Ministop. In 2014, 7-Eleven grew to more than 2,000 locations, Family Mart had nearly 1,100 stores, and Lawson had 400 locations. But perhaps no convenience store is poised to have as large an impact on Chinese consumption as the post office. Yes, you read that correctly—the post office.

Not Your Father's Post Office

It all began with a frustrated American investor, Alan Clingman, CEO of China Horizon Investment Group. Clingman has a long history in China. He had invested some money in 2006 into a small Chinese cosmetics company. This small company was selling its products through China Post, owned by the Chinese government. Through this experience, Clingman learned a great deal about China Post, a vast state-owned enterprise (SOE) that is very much part of the 800 million Chinese rural residents' everyday life.

At first, Clingman was excited to know that his company was selling its products through this massive distribution network. However, he later found out that there was no system for replenishment orders after the initial inventory was sold. He went to the China Post Office in Shandong province to learn what was happening. He asked the workers at China Post why they did not replace the order after the merchandise was sold out. The workers told him, as a matter of fact, "We are the post office. If the products are here, we will sell them. If they are gone, we just go back and sell our normal daily products. Nobody told us to reorder."

Clingman learned that, just like most state-owned company employees, they did not take initiative; they just followed orders. And nobody ever trained them that when the products are getting close to selling out, it would be time to reorder so their customers would be happy. Clingman was frustrated that China Post had this tremendous massive distribution network that would make Walmart envious, but—at the same time—the state-owned entity did not seem to care about how to best utilize the distribution network to serve its customers.

Then he found out the basic purpose of China Post Office was to distribute fertilizer, seeds, and pesticides to the hundreds of millions of farmers so that they can farm and produce income for their families. To make sure the farmers are getting their supply of agricultural products, the Chinese government started distributing those chemical products through the China Post. In order to scale the business into the village level, where most peasants live and work—most of the China Post offices are in cities and towns—China Post went to the hundreds of thousands of village general convenience store owners and asked them to join the China Post system. The owners use its brand and basically become the franchise for the village, so China Post could handle sales of stamps, payment of electric bills, and other mail products and services.

In addition, China Post told them they could sell fertilizers and other farm products to the farmers. According to Clingman's estimate, there were more than 300,000 of these types of village convenience store agents throughout China. Sometimes they were called postal stations or franchises, but primarily they were the extension of the China Post network. China Post told these franchises that the only requirement would be that everything they sold must be bought from China Post directly.

However, consumer demand has moved much faster than China Post can handle. Because China Post lacks supply-chain experience, the franchises sometimes still go elsewhere to find the products to sell to the farmers. So every day remains a challenge for the local village franchise to fulfill customer demands.

Imagine hundreds of thousands of villages throughout rural China. Each has between 2,000 and 15,000 residents waiting and looking for products to consume for their daily lives. The demand far outweighs the supply. China Post never built the supply chain to solve the problem, nor does it have the knowhow or wherewithal. Clingman saw the opportunity and initiated meetings with China Post officials. He basically told China Post "you have this massive opportunity of reaching close to one billion people. Everybody is trying to sell to a billion Chinese rural consumers, but nobody can reach them. This is a very valuable opportunity; if we combine our strengths and work together, we can build a big business together."

In 2008, after a long series of discussions and meetings with officials, Clingman and his team eventually convinced China Post to form a joint venture, called China Post Office Post Mart stores.

Creating a joint venture with one of the country's largest state-owned enterprises is no easy task and many large and successful *Fortune* companies have failed miserably. How did Clingman do it?

"First and foremost, you need to understand what China Post wants to get out of this joint venture business," Clingman says.

China Post told him that it is its mission to improve the lives of Chinese in rural areas. Further, the Chinese government wants to stimulate domestic consumption and increase it so that China will be less dependent on export, which is one of the main priorities of the twelfth Five-Year Plan.

The China Horizon CEO further explained to the China Post officials that if it collaborated with China Horizon, it could achieve all of its goals—namely, improving rural peoples' lives by bringing them better products with high-quality supply-chain management; making sure the products are genuine and safe by adhering to a higher standard; bringing rural consumers lower prices and more variety; and, above all, better service with just-in-time fulfillment.

China Post owns 50 percent of this new successful entity rather than its previous model, which was to own 100 percent of a business that was not working properly. Obviously, even though China Post Office liked the concept, as a state-owned enterprise, it had to open the opportunity for alternative companies to compete, and it had to do a great deal of analyses to evaluate the business concept before making a decision. Finally, after many rounds of discussions and negotiations, China Horizon Investment Group signed a master contract with China Post in April 2010.

The contract came after a three-year pilot program during which more than 6,000 franchised stores and 98 directly owned rural supermarkets were set up—under the Post Mart brand—in towns and villages in Shandong, Jiangxi, and Henan Provinces.

Zhang Ronglin, vice-president of China Post, says that expanding retail distribution in rural areas is a win–win for businesses and farmers.

"With the retail expertise of foreign investors, more rural residents will have the same availability and services of groceries and supermarkets as people living in the cities," he notes.

With an average shopping area ranging from 2,000 to 3,500 square feet, the rural Post Mart supermarkets will stock more than 1,000 separate items including fruit, cooking oils, and other necessities.

Wang Xiuli, a professor at the Business School of the University of International Business and Economics in Beijing, said the deal represents an excellent business opportunity as foreign retail companies tap into a neglected market with some 200 million rural households consisting of 800 million rural residents.

"The rural market is vast with a huge potential for increased consumer spending, as more migrant workers send their money home," Wang says.

With 1.3 billion people in China, the overwhelming majority of American and foreign multinationals have focused on the 500 million city dwellers, since they have higher incomes and many of them live in first- and second-tier cities like Shanghai, Beijing, Guangzhou, Suzhou, and Shenzhen. They've paid little or no attention to the 800 million rural residents who live in small villages.

These villages have rising income and people who have reached the lower-middle-class status, which means they now have aspirations to purchase foreign brands and better products for their families and children. Yet these residents lack access to most of the big-box retailers like Walmart or Carrefour, as infrastructure makes it challenging for these major retailers to deliver products to reach these residents. Besides, they are too small a market to justify building a large store (Apple will not set up a store in these villages in the foreseeable future). But China Horizon Investment Group has leveraged the trust and reach of the China Post Office, and together they have the ability to reach and serve these hundreds of millions of willing and eager consumers.

"We have more insight, data, and research on the rural Chinese consumers than anyone because of this joint venture with China Post, and today we have more than 2,000 employees," Clingman says. "Already China Post understands that China Horizon—as a private company—knows how to serve the private customers better than a state-owned enterprise, and this combines with our expertise on supply chain and our management talent."

Last-mile distribution, even for major e-commerce players like Alibaba and Taobao, is one of the biggest challenges of selling and serving China's 800 million rural customers.

"Some 88 percent of the products now sold in Post Mart are food related, but that will change as we bring in more products," Clingman says. "Our China Post Mart stores carry one-third international brands like Coke and Colgate, the other one-third are local Chinese brands like Mengniu, and the last third are our own private label products.

"And the products sold in the rural city are highly localized and seasonal, so we are attuned to the local consumers' need. China Horizon already invested $60 million in this joint venture and will be investing another $160 million in the future."

Clingman cites China Post's physical network as the joint venture's biggest advantage.

"This was a very profitable business even before we established Post Mart. China Post is the 190th most profitable company in the world with more than $4 billion of profits, versus our US Postal Service losing more than $5 billion last year. In the next three years we will expand to 10 more provinces, and in five years we will plan for an IPO in one of the China stock exchanges.

"The incomes of the Chinese rural consumers are rising fast. For example, in one region of the Henan Province, the annual family income grew from $5,000 to $12,000 from 2007 to 2012. Imagine the possibilities of supplying them all kinds of merchandise and products. For example, one of the online pharmacies in China wants to make Post Mart their drop-off point for their customers' prescription orders. And we are fast becoming the master of the last mile service even for large e-tailers and retailers."

China Horizon, along with China Post, has created 160,000 potential retail outlets and, when completed a few years from now, it will become the largest retail network in rural China. Walmart needs to watch out; it might not be the world's largest retailer for long.

Lessons Learned

- China's super consumers are everywhere and exist at all income levels. You need to look beyond the first- and second-tier cities.

- Understand your joint-venture partner's motives, leverage their strengths, and combine to serve your end customers well.
- Sometimes the Chinese state-owned enterprises are more creative than privately owned companies—be on the lookout for them, be open-minded, and find your best China partner.

Lifestyle Stores

In China, as people have transformed from consumers to super consumers, they are increasingly making purchasing decisions based on the traditional appeal of badge brands that augment *face* through conspicuous consumption. Increasingly sophisticated consumers who are no longer content to follow the herd are fueling change; they want to mark their individuality and urbanity. Some manifestations of this change include:

- Not buying the most expensive car, but one that makes a style statement.
- Seeking out niche brands.
- The rapid growth of fast-fashion retailers.
- Increased purchases of home décor.
- Increased purchases of home luxury items.
- The desire for self-expression through brand experience and aesthetic and not just value, reliability, and bling.

The increasing prominence of the lifestyle store as a channel speaks to these new desires. Retailers, brands, and manufacturers must be increasingly savvy in their responses to consumer desires by rethinking the potential of this channel.

Lifestyle stores and brands that originated in the West have realized the upside to extending their brands in China into products for which they were not initially known. Ralph Lauren, for instance, was an early mover in lifestyle. It presented its brand's rootedness in the world of White Anglo-Saxon Protestant wealth and lifestyle, and then expanded from apparel to home décor, jewelry, fragrances, and shoes.

Interestingly, some brands in China are entering and succeeding with lifestyle archetypes and exemplars that do not yet exist in China on any scale. Vans is a good example. There is little skating and rollerblading culture in China, but Chinese youth have responded to the California lifestyle and the skater look.

Specialty Retailers

Specialty retailers are also growing in importance as a modern channel—and for many of the same reasons lifestyle stores and branding are succeeding. There are a number of successful domestic specialty stores operating in China. Suning and Gome, both electronics sellers, are consistently among China's top five retailers.

Foreign companies operating specialty retail stores in China have had mixed results to date. Nike, Converse, and Li Ning are giants in the sports apparel and lifestyle market, and Sephora has met with success. Conversely, Home Depot and Best Buy failed and retreated from the market.

Multibrand Retail

While multibrand retailing has traditionally been a wasteland in China, this is starting to change. As Chinese consumers continue to travel and shop abroad, and as they spend more time and money shopping online, they are increasingly more comfortable with and enjoying the convenience of multibrand shopping.

In 2014, Lane Crawford, the Hong Kong-based women's apparel chain, expanded further into China. The venerable French department store, Galleries Lafayette (GL), also opened a flagship store in Beijing in partnership with Hong Kong company I.T. This marked the return to China for GL after opening its first store in 1995 and then closing it in 1996. Its return illustrates how much China has changed over the past 15 years and the improved prospects for multibrand retailing in China.

Chinese super consumers have fast opened up opportunities for the likes of Nordstrom, GL, and others to expand beyond their US and European bases and could change the way large scale, multibrand retailing grows in the next 10 years.

CHAPTER 15

E-commerce and the Rise of Alibaba

Q: What is the most commonly spoken language on the Internet?
A: If you answered English, you would be wrong. The answer is
Mandarin Chinese and its sister languages and dialects.

Perhaps no channel more typifies the rise and influence of China's super consumers than the massive scale, desire for, and money spent on e-commerce—including e-retail, e-wholesale, and digital information and entertainment products.

This is mainly due to the fact that the rise of retail, consumption, and brand awareness in China has been almost concurrent with the digital disruption of retail and commerce in general globally. As with many other developments in China, the lack of a legacy infrastructure meant that Chinese e-commerce could develop on a mostly blank slate without needing to tear down the old in order to make way for the new. Other examples include the ubiquity, speed, reliability, and low cost of China's mobile phone sector or the ability to build 60,000 miles of new highway without having to repair or replace the old.

While China was slower out of the gate in developing e-commerce as a key sales channel for consumer goods, it has not only caught up fast, but in many ways has surpassed the United States as the largest and most important e-commerce market in the world. The numbers are so staggering and the daily increase (yes, daily) of online shoppers is so rapid that we must acknowledge that, from the time we finish writing this chapter to the time we go to print, and then to the time you buy and read this book (approximately five months), there could be another 50 million Chinese shopping online if current trends hold.

As we go to print, there are approximately 600 million Chinese citizens with regular access to the Internet. In 2014, according to Forrester Research, a leading technology research and consulting firm based in the United States, by the end of 2014 there will be more than 350 million active online shoppers in China, spending $294 billion—and that number may rise to 600 million spending more than $600 billion by 2017.

To put those numbers in perspective: The United States is the third most populous country on earth (after China and India) at 320 million people, yet China has more online shoppers today than America has people. Changes in business, technology, and culture in China happen in dog years. What often takes five to seven years to happen in more developed markets will usually happen in a year or less in China. This is especially true of e-commerce.

Alibaba

You cannot talk about e-commerce in China without first talking about Alibaba. Founded in 1999 by former English teacher Jack Ma, Alibaba started life as a business-to-business platform. It was essentially a place where thousands of Chinese manufacturers could advertise their wares and provide contact details for foreign buyers. It was the perfect company and idea for its era, as the company was founded just prior to China joining the World Trade Organization, and hundreds of thousands of companies went to China looking to make and buy manufactured products.

These makers and buyers found a virtual meeting place. Alibaba in some ways was the earliest confluence of three of the biggest business stories of the 90s: the rise of China, the rise of e-commerce, and a world shrunk by modern supply chains. Where once the twice-yearly Canton Fair trade and manufacturing show in Guangzhou was the only place to find partners and make deals, Alibaba quickly emerged as a 24/7, year-round Canton Fair.

Japan's Softbank invested $20 million early and Yahoo! later bought half the company (it now owns 22 percent after a sell-back). As we go to print, Alibaba has filed for its initial public offering (IPO) in the United States, which is scheduled for August 8, 2014. It is possible that, by the time you are reading this, Alibaba will have become one of the largest tech IPOs, if not the largest IPO in history. It is estimated the offering will raise $10 to $15 billion. And it is quite possible that number will be dwarfed come IPO day. Today, the dollar value of items sold through the three biggest e-commerce companies in the world on a dollar value of goods sold per year, according to Alibaba's IPO filing are as follows: Alibaba ($248 billion), Amazon ($100 billion), and eBay ($76 billion). Alibaba has sold twice Amazon's total and three times eBay's total—and there are another 600 million Chinese who don't even use the Internet regularly, yet.

How did a start-up, business-to-business company, founded in Hangzhou, become one of the decade's most talked about and eagerly anticipated IPOs? It moved its focus to e-commerce. Alibaba 2.0 again became the perfect company for its time in China. When China's initial consumer boom started gaining steam in the mid- to late 2000s, e-commerce played a relatively insignificant role. Chinese consumers were focused on bricks and mortar stores where they could see, touch, experience, and haggle over the prices of the products they wanted.

When eBay, Amazon, and other Western e-commerce companies entered China during this period, Chinese companies, and Alibaba more than any other, took notice of the potential of e-commerce in China. There has been a lot written and discussed about why eBay and other Western companies never found a major market in China. We are not here to argue whether it was a case of bad decisions and lack of understanding or internal Chinese mechanisms that made it difficult for them to do business. Perhaps the best summary of the case came from Jack Ma himself when he said, "eBay is a shark in the ocean. We are a crocodile in the Yangtze River. If we fight in the ocean, we will lose. But if we fight in the river, we will win."

In other words, Alibaba could adopt the foundational ideas and technological infrastructures of Western e-commerce, but its natural advantage lay in being Chinese, thinking Chinese, and serving Chinese. Through a combination of e-commerce tailored for the Chinese mind-set, culture, language, and purchase motivators, along with legitimate technological advances and the abandonment of the playing field by foreign competitors—Alibaba became not only the biggest e-commerce player in China, but also the world.

The company today is Amazon, eBay, Etsy, Digital Mall, and PayPal all rolled into one. Alibaba now plays a part in nearly 80 percent of all online purchases in China. Tao Bao, founded in 2003, is the company's consumer-to-consumer marketplace where millions of Chinese sell to each other every day. A great Tao Bao innovation was to introduce Ali Wang Wang, which allows buyers and sellers to talk and negotiate in real time through instant messaging. This feature resulted from understanding the importance of trust and personal relationships in Chinese commercial interactions (as opposed to the purely transactional and commercial e-commerce models of the West).

Tmall, created in 2010, is the company's business-to-consumer platform. It is the place where domestic and foreign brands sell their products directly to Chinese consumers. There are currently more than 75,000 brands and 60,000 merchants on Tmall. Consumers can find everything from Tory Burch handbags, to Crest toothpaste, to parts for locally produced Cherry automobiles.

Everything on Tao Bao and Tmall can be paid for using Ali Pay, the PayPal-like escrow service. Alibaba has also branched out into cloud computing, streaming media, and venture capital. But for now it is the most important name in Chinese e-commerce, embraced, loved, and used by nearly 300 million consumers. With the IPO, the company is also setting its sights on foreign expansion; the company has launched its first US venture—11Main.com—a platform that will allow small merchants and artisans to sell their products to a wider audience.

Regardless, brands, retailers, and anyone hoping to engage Chinese consumers must utilize, in some form, Alibaba and its multiple platforms —just ask the National Football League.

NFL Footballs "Sold Out"

The National Football League (NFL) is America's most popular sports league. Comprising 32 franchises that compete each year to win the Super Bowl, the world's biggest annual sporting event, the NFL has developed the model for the successful modern sports league. This includes extensive revenue sharing, competitive excellence, strong franchises across the board, and national distribution. The NFL is the industry leader on a wide range of fronts. But the National Basketball Association (NBA) has been the real success story for US-based sports leagues in China. NBA basketball is the second most popular team sport in China after soccer. The NBA invested early and heavily in understanding Chinese, and the NFL would like to take a page from the NBA playbook by expanding its influence to China. And to demonstrate its long-term commitment to China, while signifying a significant milestone in the NFL's continuing effort to promote its game worldwide, the league established NFL China in October 2007.

In China, the NFL aims to develop and grow its fan base by increasing fan passion for the game through strategic cooperation with national and regional media partners. Marketing efforts focus on flag-football development and fan-outreach events, as well as a strong social media presence. Today the NFL has more than 3 million avid fans in China. However, in a country with 1.3 billion people, that is a tiny number—not nearly large enough to justify playing an NFL game in China. By comparison, NBA China has more than 1 million fans and more than 60 million followers on social media sites like Sina and Tencent, according to David Shoemaker, CEO of NBA China.

Even with such a tiny fan base, NFL China has deployed one of our China rules for success: Take a jab at the China super consumer and land a right hook through e-commerce.

NFL China partners with more than 25 regional TV broadcasters and digital media outlets across China to air weekly games, highlights, and other NFL content. Additionally, NFL China focuses on grassroots development of football through the University Flag Football League, with teams competing from 36 universities across Beijing, Shanghai, and Guangzhou. In 2013, the NFL established NFL home fields in those cities. This brought together a number of elements that fans appreciate in the United States, such as a full day of football, as well as community engagement that includes live football games, interactive games, training clinics, food, drinks, and appearances by NFL players and cheerleaders.

But still, how can the NFL sell to the China super consumer when there is virtually no brand recognition? Here comes the right hook! Amazon.com is not the largest e-commerce company in the world, Alibaba is. By some measures, Alibaba Tmall.com, Alibaba's business-to-consumer unit, has grown to become one of, if not the most, important e-commerce platforms in the world.

Why should the NFL care about Chinese super consumers and Tmall.com, when it is doing so well in America? Because, according to a recent study published by *Focus Money* magazine, Chinese consumers shop online 8.4 times each month, compared to 5.2 times in the United States, 4.3 times in Great Britain, 2.9 times in Germany, 2.8 times in the Netherlands, 2.6 times in France, and 2.3 times in Switzerland.

November 11, 2014, was China's "singles-day" shopping festival and Alibaba alone generated more than $5.1 billion in revenue … in one day, more than the total online sales in the United States on Black Friday and Cyber Monday combined.

Enter Frank Lavin, who hopes to build the longer, wider bridge American and European companies need in order access and succeed in Chinese e-commerce. Lavin is well qualified for the job of bridge builder. He served as US ambassador to Singapore; led trade negotiations with China while working at the US Department of Commerce; held senior posts in the Asian offices of Bank of America and Citibank; and worked at the public-relations giant Edelman. In other words, Frank is a master of *Guanxi* (good relationships).

Leveraging his contacts, Lavin raised several million dollars in angel money and established Export Now, an Ohio- and Shanghai-based company, with 30 employees, providing turnkey solutions for American companies on Tmall.com.

When NFL China approached Frank to set up its store on Tmall.com, it had no idea whether there would be demand. Unlike more established products and brand categories, it is difficult to conduct research in order to gauge demand for NFL-licensed products. It is a bit like trying to predict demand for Starbucks' coffee in 1980, when China was still strictly a tea-drinking nation. Spending hundreds of thousands of dollars for a feasibility study would not work in this situation.

Lavin suggested that the NFL send the smallest possible shipment of NFL footballs to China as a test. So the NFL sent a single pallet of six dozen footballs. The cost of shipping all 72 footballs was less than a plane ticket to Beijing. This market test was extremely inexpensive to conduct. The idea was that even a very small demand would be significant considering the market's overall size.

The footballs sold out in less than three minutes. But Export Now still couldn't measure how big the market really was. So NFL China then sent a larger shipment of 288 footballs. And again, they quickly sold out.

Encouraged by the demand, the NFL has built a full e-commerce store, which went live in October 2013.

Why E-commerce?

The value of e-commerce through Tmall.com is the low cost and the fact that a brand can move incrementally and scale up when it sees a positive demand. And because of the low-cost structure compared to opening an actual office and hiring full-time employees, the downside is small. In just a few years, Export Now has built more than 110 branded storefronts shops on its Tmall.com store, which showcases only American products.

A recent study by Boston Consulting Group indicates that more than half of all Chinese consumers prefer American products to Chinese products. Because Chinese super consumers will pay more for American-made products, not only do brands not have to sacrifice their profit margins, they can also often charge a premium price for their products.

Another company taking advantage of the Export Now platform is Totes. Headquartered in Cincinnati, Totes Isotoner Corporation makes umbrellas, gloves, rainwear, rubber overshoes, and other weather-related accessories. In June 2013, Export Now set up the Totes online store, which sells a full line of company products and complements the brand's existing presence in traditional retail channels throughout China.

"The increasing popularity of our products in retail markets in China prompted us to look for a way to expand our capability to reach more consumers in the second-largest economy in the world," said Douglas Gernert, chief executive officer of the Totes Isotoner Corporation. "Export Now provided an online marketing solution that is perfect for our needs, and we expect the new online store to be a key contributor to our ongoing growth in this important venue for us."

Lavin adds that Chinese online shoppers are hungry for greater access to high-quality consumer brands like Totes.

"This vast, profitable, and largely untapped marketplace is ripe for companies seeking new opportunities to grow their global sales and expand the reach of their products," he says.

While Alibaba may be the biggest e-commerce player in China, they are hardly alone. JD.com, formerly 360buy.com, is a fierce rival, holding

17 percent market share. They have shifted focus to the m-commerce (mobile commerce) market. Mobile is the preferred method to access the Internet in China today and more and more purchases are being conducted through the phone. JD is expected to go public soon as well, and they are rumored to be working on an Amazon/Facebook-type hybrid.

There are challenges to utilizing e-commerce channels in China, and they must be dealt with and planned for well in advance of entering the marketplace. For brands and retailers these challenges include:

- Fierce competition and a crowded marketplace.
- Confusion about what platforms are available and best suited to their needs.
- Finding the right mix of third-party platforms, owned and operated e-commerce platforms, and consumer-generated commerce.
- Assuming you can enter and succeed in China with an e-commerce-only plan.
- Supply chain infrastructure, especially warehousing, e-fulfillment, cross-country shipping, and last-mile delivery.
- Controlling intellectual property (IP), parallel imports, and gray-market issues.

This last challenge is particularly difficult and sometimes costly, both in terms of revenues lost and brand identity erosion.

China law expert Dan Harris, author of the influential and award-winning China Law Blog, says, "Companies who are selling in China need to make registration of their trademarks, copyrights, and other intellectual property their first priority." He continues, "China is a first-to-file country, not first to use, so whether you are selling or making something in China, without up-front IP due diligence and action, it is not a matter of *if* you will get infringed upon, but *when*. The danger is exponentially worse online. Our lawyers spend a good chunk of their time trying to remedy IP infringements generated though e-commerce, but many companies are learning that spending on prevention is cheaper than spending on remedies," said Harris.

Let's be clear, explicit, and blunt: If you put your products up for sale online in China and you have not registered your trademarks, copyrights, and all other IP in China, **You no longer own it**. Someone else does.

What are they buying? Trying to track what Chinese consumers buy the most online is similar to trying to keep an accurate and up-to-date list on their preferred travel destinations; in other words, very difficult. That said, while particular brands or products bought can shift quickly, the major categories bought are, for now, fairly stable. These include:

- Apparel and fashion accessories
- Household items
- Personal care and healthcare products
- Sports and recreation products
- Consumer electronics

Interestingly, while China's e-commerce spending and luxury spending are both outsized, only a tiny proportion, less than 5 percent, of luxury purchases are made online. This has a lot to do with the percentage of luxury items bought offshore, but concerns about fakes, the experience of luxury shopping in the offline world, and the desire to touch and feel the workmanship of luxury items also play major roles. It will be up to China's e-commerce platforms and brands to work together to make the two intersect more in the future.

Today, marketplaces like Tao Bao, Tmall, JD.com, Xiu.com, and others account for the majority of e-tail sales in China, with a handful of key categories dominating the product mix. Additionally, the majority of sales are still made through PCs, laptops, and tablets.

But the trend lines are clear: mobile will be *the* dominant technology for e-commerce; joint-venture sites for hypermarkets, like Walmart and Carrefour, will grow; more companies will mix their own China-based e-commerce, tablet commerce, and mobile commerce sites with platforms and other multibrand retail channels, as the department store Lane Crawford did.

As the post-cultural revolution generation of first-time capitalists, entrepreneurs, merchants, and consumers pass the reins of business leadership to the generation born in the 1980s and 1990s—many of whom have been educated overseas but returned home for the opportunity to take over or create their own businesses—the pace of innovation and growth at the intersection of technology and commerce will be further energized, and an Internet with Chinese characteristics will become more influential on a global basis.

In a country where digital disruption is less disruption and more native environment and—in a China that was able to skip over several twentieth-century retail models—the digital consumption of products, services, and entertainment by Chinese consumers will further the need for foreign and domestic Chinese companies to understand and cater to the China market, as well as the China global demographic.

The growth of Chinese e-tail, combined with the continued growth of business-to-business and wholesale digital commerce in China, will have a profound effect on the way brands, retailers, information technology companies, web-property developers, supply chain service providers, as well as research and consulting firms do business over the next 10 years. But, as with anything else in China, the winners and losers will most often be separated by who best understands Chinese history, culture, language, and mind-set along with the desires and prerogatives of the Chinese government.

CHAPTER 16

Supply Chains to Satisfy China's Super Consumers

China's super consumers offer businesses an enormous economic opportunity on the mainland, in Greater China, overseas, and online, but as the China Post example in the previous chapter illustrates, it also presents one of the most difficult challenges for supply chains. We can't say this too often or too emphatically—*the companies who succeed with Chinese consumers are the companies who master their global, China, regional, and local supply chains.*

For more than 25 years, *supply chain,* in China, meant manufacturing products and exporting them to other countries. The Chinese consumer was an afterthought, if a thought at all, as the country lived up to its reputation as the factory of the world. But all of this has changed since China emerged as the largest consumer market in the world. As the Chinese consumer continues to grow more sophisticated, supply chains will need to match (and even exceed) this rate of change and focus on end-to-end operations in the same manner as the most successful global companies.

Retail and consumer product operations driven by e-commerce are transforming rapidly, and China is no exception.

How can supply chains improve to meet this huge new challenge? Tompkins International is a global supply-chain consulting firm, based in Raleigh, North Carolina. The company has its Asian headquarters in Shanghai. There are two divisions in the Shanghai office, the market strategy and implementation practice, which Michael leads, and the supply-chain practice group. Tompkins has helped shape the global supply-chain industry over the past 35 years and was an early entrant in providing supply-chain strategies and implementation for foreign and domestic companies in China.

According to Jim Tompkins, CEO of Tompkins International, "Companies selling to Chinese consumers on the Mainland, in Greater China, and in the West must now consider their approach to all six megaprocesses of the supply chain. This is especially true in e-fulfillment, as China has become the largest e-commerce market in the world."

Supply Chain Megaprocesses

Tompkins continues, "To succeed, supply chains in China will need to move from a primary focus on manufacturing and exporting to a whole new definition that encompasses the megaprocesses of *plan—buy—make—store—distribute—sell*."

If a company deals with products, it must have capabilities for plan—buy—make—store—distribute—sell, whether it performs these processes in house or outsources to selected service providers. Further, it needs basic capabilities for support, such as information technology, back-office functions, HR, sales, and marketing.

Investing more time and energy into supply-chain strategy will ensure that your business model will adapt to the changing role of China from factory floor to booming global marketplace. The real key for supply chains will be not only producing good products, but moving these products quickly through the megaprocesses while having visibility, being able to forecast demand, and ensuring product replenishment and fulfillment.

The best example we can provide for success through supply-chain strategy in China is the Italian men's luxury apparel company, Ermenegildo Zegna. Zegna entered China almost 25 years ago. The company was patient in its approach to success in China. It opened stores slowly, took incremental steps informed by the nature and needs of the market, and invested heavily in brand identity. Of course, providing the best-quality materials, products, and superb service undergirded all of this. The Zegna suit became an early marker of success for Chinese men. Although Zegna had been successful in China for many years, it was through rethinking its supply chain strategy, infrastructure, and deployment that it became the best-selling men's luxury apparel brand in China.

Zegna focused on reducing inventory, increasing sell-through, and boosting the bottom line through supply chain. By applying science, analytics, and best practices across all six megaprocesses—and fusing that with the art of understanding the differences in Chinese market clusters, climates, and tastes—in fewer than three years Zegna grew revenue five-fold. This brings up a general point for established and new brands and retailers in China. It is no longer enough to not only show up, or be smart, but to have an e-fulfillment, warehouse, planning, transportation, and replenishment program that separates you from your competition. The following is a breakdown of how the right understanding and implementation of a supply chain will lead to success with Chinese consumers.

Plan

Multiple paths exist to establish, design, and execute the flow of goods, information, cash, and work across supply chains, from suppliers to customers. Markets and customers within China can be different from the Western world, but the product planning process must be similar to reach the newest, savviest consumers.

The primary purpose of supply-chain planning is the synchronization of supply with demand. Supply-chain planning at the operational level addresses:

- How to forecast demand for your products.
- How to meet this demand.
- How to best supply the products to the right place, at the right time, and at the right price.
- How to do all this in the most cost-effective manner.

The total delivered cost of any product to any customer in China must be competitive with other product sources. Supply-chain planning also provides for the right strategies. Decisions on outsourcing logistics services are basic to the strategy, as are decisions about the design of the logistics network.

In addition, supply-chain planning addresses important tangential issues such as taxes. The flow and storage of goods, as well as the locations of facilities, are major determinants of Chinese taxes.

Buy

Poor product quality, erratic supply, and a higher total cost of ownership are some of the frustrations traditionally experienced within supply chains in China. To ensure that your company is equipped to succeed for the long term, consider these guiding questions:

- What is your strategy for sourcing, purchasing, supplier relationship management, and procurement IT?
- What processes are needed to execute this strategy?
- What talent in your organization is astute enough about China to execute your strategy?
- What type of technology currently supports the operations, and is it robust enough for China operations?
- What performance measurement metrics do you use to ensure success?

Make

This is the megaprocess that has been most associated with China in the past few decades. Manufacturing within Asia can provide a competitive edge in pricing, quality, and overall cost of doing business. But unless you follow the right strategic processes, your savings could become liabilities. It is advisable to take a macro-level evaluation of the trends and influences that will affect your company's current and future manufacturing decisions in Asia. This is more important than ever as companies shift from making in China for export to "China for China" manufacturing.

Conduct an internal audit of goals, capabilities, and desired results for your company's manufacturing and sourcing plans. In addition, plan external audits to identify issues with current suppliers and to pinpoint potential new suppliers. Facilities, management, processes, QC standards, and workers should all be vetted. Negotiate the most advantageous terms for price, payment, and standards regarding contracts, purchase orders, and shipping. This applies whether you are making products in China, in your home country, or in a third-party country. China's super consumers have created an environment where the decision of where to make (China, the United States, Europe, Mexico, South America, or some combination) is not as clear-cut as it used to be.

For example, some companies we have worked with have been high on moving production to Mexico to save on per unit costs, only to have us show them that their second-largest market in two years will be China and they will need to ship goods back, or that their raw materials and component supply chains are still in China and those will need to be shipped to Mexico.

Distribute

No process in your China supply chain is more important than the physical movement of products from their point of origin to point of consumption. At the same time, no country with this large of a consumer market faces such substantial transportation issues.

China's distribution infrastructure is still relatively undeveloped, and modern, Western best practices and facilities are just now becoming prominent.

Leading companies, like Zegna, have shifted focus to demand-driven supply chains that deliver the right products on time, in the right quantities, at the right price. Determining and implementing the optimal international commercial terms (incoterms), complying with global trade policies and regulations, assessing and managing risks, and analyzing cost/service trade-offs for each transport mode can mean the difference between success and failure.

Even the best-planned transportation strategy must be managed closely to ensure that what is supposed to happen actually happens. Performance monitoring, from receipt of a purchase order through to shipment delivery, requires end-to-end visibility.

The rapid growth of China's retail and consumer-goods markets presents companies with a host of supply-chain challenges, especially those companies seeking to evolve into managers of their own distribution networks, capable of fueling organic growth in Asia. It is critical to implement distribution centers that are more sophisticated, flexible, designed for growth, and cost conscious. There is no other way to meet ever-changing customer demands.

Sell

A supply chain's primary purpose is to meet (and even expand) customer demand for a company's products in a cost-effective manner. This is just as true in China as anywhere else, as consumers increasingly seek quality products at competitive prices. Post-sales service for certain products is an obvious inclusion in your China supply chains, but one that many companies leave out and then have to catch up on, after damage to the brand due to poor service has already happened. Effective customer service also involves product positioning, fulfillment, and even in-store activities for retail.

Super consumers in China expect more and will not be satisfied without service levels that focus on their needs. Designing demand-driven supply chains within China is just as important as in the West; the difference is in knowing the customers and their preferences—along with having a customer program that designates ordering, buying, and receiving product service as points of satisfaction.

Aligning Strategy, Structure, and Implementation

Planning and executing all the supply-chain megaprocesses (plan—buy—make—store—distribute—sell) means involving suppliers all the way through to the end customers. Alignment brings together supply-chain strategies, processes, people, and technologies, as well as facility designs and material handling integrations.

Let's look at each part—strategy, structure, and implementation—and its function within a modern Chinese consumer product supply chain.

1. Strategy

Business strategy defines current and future products that the company sells, the China markets in which they sell, and the value proposition, why people buy from them. Operations strategy defines the operational capabilities and operating model that the company needs. In today's complex China few initiatives are implemented effectively or meet expectations, since they are not structured to address the entirety of the business objectives. Companies in China must ensure their operations' strategy is well defined, is in perfect alignment with the business strategy, and has gained consensus on the path forward as well as the priorities to be achieved.

2. **Structure**

These are the end-to-end supply chain processes and capabilities required to accomplish goals and objectives defined by the operations strategy. Operational capabilities depend on the right policies, as well as the ways that the operating model leverages people, processes, and technology. Today, it is not always about optimizing costs in the supply chain, but also to have the policies, processes, and infrastructure that meet the cost objectives (total cost to serve) and support the service goals that will drive sales. These policies, processes, and infrastructure can be dramatically different in China and we recommend a complete rethink, rather than trying to force your current model into China.

3. **Implementation**

This is defined as how well all supply-chain components function to achieve acceptance within the day-to-day operations of the company and how well they meet performance targets. Effective program and project management are critical success factors in China, just as they are around the world. Experience managing and coordinating many internal and external organizations, addressing the organizational change required, and achieving project objectives on time and under budget are capabilities that define a successful supply-chain implementation team. Overall, alignment of operations with strategies enhances business performance and bridges the gap between planning and execution.

CHAPTER 17

Segmentation

It is not our differences that divide us. It is our inability to recognize, accept, and celebrate those differences.

—Audre Lorde

After defining the Chinese super consumer—and coming to understand the fact that there is both a China market and a China Global Demographic Market—it is important that we further define Chinese consumers by way of segmentation. How can you possibly know which of the more than 1 billion consumers are potentially yours?

Surveying China

When it comes to studying and analyzing the demographic tapestry that is the China super consumer, the global consulting firm McKinsey & Company sets the standard. It has been conducting annual consumer surveys in China since 2005, with more than 60,000 people in over 60 Chinese cities interviewed so far. Surveying in China is not an easy task, due to its vast geography, but McKinsey has gained tremendous insights on Chinese consumers' income growth, shifting spending patterns, and rising expectations, and they are different from their American counterparts. These surveys provide a better understanding of the different consumer segments and how they've grown.

Gordon Orr has been the chairman of Asia for McKinsey since 1996 and he is responsible for McKinsey's client services in the region. Orr opened McKinsey's office in Beijing and led McKinsey's Greater

China practice for many years. In addition, he has led McKinsey's strategy and technology practices in Asia. Orr has served on McKinsey's global board of directors since 2003 and has been with McKinsey since 1986. He works with leading Asian companies, mainly in North Asia, on large transformational programs that combine perspectives from strategy, operations, leadership, and technology. Currently, he leads McKinsey's research that focuses on the globalization of Asian enterprises, and he sits on the board of the McKinsey Technology Institute, the firm's think tank on long-term technology trends. He spoke to us at length about China's super consumers and segmentation.

"The nature of Chinese consumers is changing very rapidly, and the outdated concept of lumping all Chinese consumers into one bucket that is looking for low-cost everything is dying very fast," Orr explains. "A significant segment of Chinese consumers are value driven. However, the new mainstream Chinese consumers—those who have income levels from $15,000 to $30,000 per year—have become the sweet spot of Chinese consumption and they do things differently. To start, they shop less frequently but spend larger amounts. They are more sophisticated and they are willing to trade up to get what they want. They are also incredibly shaped by what they read on the Internet. And, increasingly, they buy on the Internet as well."

Orr adds: "This generation of Chinese consumers is growing up with the Internet and close to 20 percent make their purchases on their mobile phones. When they see the products in retail stores they want to see if they can buy them cheaper online. They are looking for information and pricing comparisons on the Internet. In the luxury sector, Chinese consumers already account for 27 percent of worldwide purchases. It will grow to 34 percent by 2015."

According to Orr, McKinsey's insight provides a window into what Chinese consumption will look like five years from now. Sophistication is taking hold with remarkable speed among more seasoned Chinese luxury consumers, those who have been buying luxury for some time. As we noted in Chapter 16, these Chinese consumers increasingly tend to shun flashy products in favor of products with understated styles. To distinguish themselves from traditional new Chinese buyers, they like to discover smaller and niche brands, ever-more luxurious items, or rare one-of-a-kind offerings.

At the same time, there is continued growth in the number of consumers who have only recently reached income levels at which designer labels are affordable. These new entrants to the luxury market tend to purchase products that clearly display their newfound status, often from brands that are widely recognizable. With both groups growing rapidly, the market is diversifying and luxury-goods makers face more complicated choices about tailoring their products to the various segments of Chinese consumers.

Changes in Chinese consumers' economic profiles will continue to be the most important trend shaping the consumer landscape. The Chinese are certainly getting richer faster. Per-capita disposable income of urban consumers will reach approximately $8,000; it was $4,000 in 2010. That number is close to the current standard of living in South Korea, but still far from that in the United States (approximately $35,000) and Japan (approximately $26,000).

Orr's team at McKinsey has also found that the great majority of Chinese population, at present, consists of value consumers (those living in households with annual disposable income between $6,000 and $16,000, which is just about enough to cover their basic needs). Mainstream consumers (relatively wealthy households with annual disposable income between $16,000 and $34,000) form a very small group by comparison (less than 14 million such households, representing only 6 percent of the urban population). A smaller group of affluent consumers, whose household income exceeds $34,000, comprise only 2 percent of the urban population, or 4.26 million households; still, that is almost 15 million people.

Until now, these divergences have presented multinational companies operating in China a choice: Either target mainstream and affluent consumers exclusively, or extend their brands to serve value consumers.

Those that took the first course were more or less able to maintain the business model they applied in other parts of the world without needing to reengineer their products. But in so doing, they were limited to a target market of 18 million households. Companies that chose to serve the value category have had a much bigger market in which to play (184 million households), but their products have had to be cheaper and they have had to adapt their business models. As a result, profitability has been lower.

"This situation is changing," Orr says. "Because the wealth of so many consumers is rising so rapidly, many value consumers will have joined the mainstream by 2020. Mainstream consumers will then account for 51 percent of the urban population. Although their absolute level of wealth will still be quite low compared with that of consumers in developed countries, this group—comprising 167 million households or close to 400 million people—will become the standard setters for consumption with the ability to afford family cars and small luxury items. American companies can respond by introducing better-quality products to a vast group of new consumers, differentiating themselves from competitors and earning higher profits."

He adds that "value consumers, reduced to 36 percent of urban households in 2020 from 82 percent in 2010, will still represent an enormous market for cheaper products: 116 million households or 307 million consumers. Affluent consumers will remain an elite minority, making up only 6 percent of the Chinese population in 2020. But that 6 percent will translate into about 21 million affluent households, or 60 million affluent consumers."

Orr also discourages the common practice of grouping Chinese consumers into tiers based on the relative prosperity and development of particular cities. Instead, he suggests mapping China's market into different clusters.

"The China clustering, in my opinion, is counterintuitive, when you try to market to Chinese consumers," Orr says. "Most companies go to China by segmenting their products into tier-1 or tier-2 or tier-3 cities. We believe managing growth in China using clusters can help better leverage economies of scale and prioritize initiatives more effectively."

McKinsey divides China into 22 city clusters, which represent 92 percent of China's urban GDP in 2015, cover 611 cities, and account for 86 percent of the population. If you market to six or seven connected cities, it would be far more effective than to market to different tiers of cities in China.

"There are more things in common among those clusters than various cities in the same tier, so it would be both easy and more effective to target them accordingly," Orr says. "The benefits of using clusters are significant cost savings across cities within the same cluster as well as the brand halo effect through shared media across common regions and through exposure where people may work or travel but don't live.

Besides, distribution and sales-force efficiency would be easier to manage in neighboring cities in the cluster. Last but not least, there will be superior supply-chain efficiencies driven by geographic proximity."

In six of China's 22 city clusters—Shanghai, Nanjing, Changchun-Harbin, Liao Central South, and Chongqing—20 percent of the population will be over the age of 65 by 2020. But in five other clusters—Guangzhou, Shenzhen, Nanning, Kunming, and Fuzhou-Xiamen—the majority will be under 34. Several reasons account for this: Some clusters have attracted large numbers of young migrants looking for what is mainly labor-intensive work; others are poorer, so life expectancy is lower; and in some regions, the one-child policy was not strictly enforced.

Orr believes that the gradual aging of the population in certain clusters, like Shanghai, will become an increasingly critical component in formulating an effective marketing strategy.

"The senior market is not mature today in China," Orr says. "Most people in China over the age of 55 experienced the harsh conditions of the Cultural Revolution in the late 1960s and early 1970s. Not surprisingly, they do not spend frivolously. Among residents of tier-one cities, 55- to 65-year-old residents allocate half of their expenditure to food and little to discretionary categories. Only 7 percent of their spending goes toward apparel, for example. In comparison, those who are 10 years younger spend only 38 percent on food but 13 percent on apparel."

Orr adds that "consumer surveys have revealed that although today's older consumers behave very differently from younger people, today's 45- to 54-year-olds—the older generation come 2020—demonstrate spending patterns similar to those of 34- to 45-year-olds (who allocate 34 percent of their spending to food and 14 percent to apparel). This implies that companies will have to rethink their notion of older consumers."

China's aging demographic means that, as a share of the total population, there will be 5 percent more people above the age of 65 in 2020 than there are today. That is an additional 126.5 million Chinese senior citizens, clearly an important consumer segment. But what is equally important is the way in which the spending patterns of older people in 2020 will differ from those of older people now.

The pronounced variations shown in McKinsey's survey—whereby older people were more inclined to save and less willing to spend on discretionary items such as travel, leisure, and nice clothes—are likely to be much less apparent in 2020.

While Orr's observation points to a more robust spending culture as the China super consumer population ages and becomes wealthier, the way he or she goes about making purchases will not change very much. Pragmatism, including the emphasis on value, quality, and intense product research, is deeply ingrained in the Chinese mind-set and is here to stay.

A Most Discerning Consumer

Before deciding what they might buy, most Chinese consumers allocate a budget, evaluate the features and worthwhile benefits, and then they hunt down the best bargains. Impulse purchases are not common (28 percent of people admit to buying on impulse, compared with 49 percent in the United Kingdom). These attitudes and behaviors are influenced by traditional Confucian values, and they are deeply rooted in the Chinese mind-set. We do not see a forthcoming shift in attitudes towards spending. Certainly, consumption will rise strongly in line with rapid income growth, and savings rates may well fall. In the end, though, the Chinese will remain smart shoppers because they are willing to spend time researching purchases. Further, with price comparisons easier to make on the Internet, they may become smarter still.

For example, today, 48 percent of Chinese consumers seek value for money as one of their top five considerations when purchasing a mobile phone, compared with 20 percent in 2009. Not only will the Chinese super consumer continue to perform serious due diligence, but he or she will have more tools with which to work—and the in-store point of sale will likely experience some decline.

In the past decade, the Chinese have embraced modern retail formats, treating shopping as a form of entertainment for the entire family rather than just a necessity. The next decade will expose many new consumers to the experience, especially migrant workers and residents of smaller cities. Trips to malls will lose their novelty, partly because other leisure activities will be on offer, owing to government efforts to boost the entertainment industry and private consumption. Novelty value in shopping will lie instead with e-commerce. Fast-changing lifestyles in densely populated cities are strengthening shoppers' demands for convenience. Increasingly, e-commerce will satisfy that demand.

According to McKinsey, by 2020, 14 to 15 percent of retail sales will take place online and, in certain categories such as consumer electronics, that ratio could be as high as 30 to 40 percent. For groceries, the current figure of less than 1 percent could move closer to the current level of about 10 percent in the United States. Rapid development of shopping applications on mobile devices, online payment systems, and logistics infrastructure will fuel the growth of e-commerce by enhancing convenience and security. The Chinese could become among the most sophisticated online shoppers in the world.

As we have highlighted, China and Chinese consumers are not monoliths that share the same needs, levels of sophistication, spending habits, priorities, and resources. So whom exactly are we talking about?

A good place to start is age. As Orr notes, Chinese super consumers are still young—in some cases, very young—relative to other markets. For example, the average luxury consumer in China is 39 years old as opposed to 59 years old in the United States. We have seen luxury companies enter China and fail because they were addressing their traditional 49 to 69 demographic when in reality their potential customers were 29 to 49 years old. They were not advertising in the right media, they underestimated the importance of social media, and they did not understand the importance of peer-to-peer endorsement. In some cases we have seen that their entire messaging strategy and appeal were geared toward a generation that had little interest in the brand.

CHAPTER 18

Marketing

Half the money I spend on advertising is wasted; the trouble is, I don't know which half.

—John Wanamaker

When the first television ads for automobiles starting appearing on China Central Television (CCTV) in the 1980s, a typical ad would consist of a picture of a car, superimposed on a blue background, and some white copy that would typically read: "We are now selling Toyota (or Volkswagen). If you are interested, please call this phone number."

Until the late 1980s and early 1990s, billboards in Chinese cities were almost exclusively the domain of the Party and included slogans, news, and inspiration. Print was the exclusive domain of state-owned newspapers, journals, and proto-magazines with no physical or ideological room for advertising consumer products. Radio, like television, was state owned and also off limits to advertisers.

Today things could not be more different. Advertising-supported media of every kind have exploded and proliferated in every corner of China over the past 15 years. There are thousands of TV stations, tens of thousands of radio stations and programs, thousands of newspapers and magazines, brand-touting billboards on every corner, and, more recently, electronic displays of every shape and size everywhere, from taxis to elevators to the sides of buildings. This is to say nothing of the Internet and its tens of millions of points of contact with consumers.

According to Scott Markman, CEO of The Monogram Group, a Chicago/Shanghai advertising and marketing firm that for 10 years has been actively and successfully helping Chinese and American companies sell on both sides of the ocean, the development of a broad and deep media landscape in China over the past 20 years has been instrumental in creating and informing the tastes of China's consumers. The circular-feedback loop, where consumption fuels media and advertising, and media and advertising feed consumption, has been one of modern China's hallmarks. Companies hoping to connect with and engage Chinese consumers must clearly understand the channels for marketing in China and also how to use those channels to create emotional and personal connections.

Chinese consumers are very brand-aware but not very brand-loyal, just as they are very price-aware but also, in many cases, not price-sensitive. Here we provide an overview of marketing to Chinese consumers, the channels that are available, and some examples of companies and brands that have succeeded (or failed) in marketing to Chinese consumers on a local, national, and global basis.

Consumer Impulses and Desires

In many ways China's super consumers have adopted the *gotta-have-it* mind-set as more consumers (especially those under 50) come into discretionary income and even generational wealth. Many Chinese citizens have been asking themselves: "Why should I follow the cultural tradition of sacrifice and modest means, when I can afford a consumer and brand lifestyle that I see many of my friends pursuing as well?" "How can I acquire instant status?" "How do I let others know who I am?"

Markman continues, "This first played out among wealthy entrepreneurs and their families in purchasing luxury goods, with a love of badge brands during the consumer boom years of the 2000s. We see this in the desire to drive a Porsche, wear a Prada purse, or order a Remy Martin XO cognac in a bar."

Markman adds: "This same phenomenon is trickling down to Chinese domestic brands as well now. As China's collective confidence and self-image rises and as more Chinese brands acquire worldwide distribution, so will the perception that status and prestige can be acquired with products from Chinese brands."

Lenovo's Approach: The Best of Both Worlds

If more Chinese do gravitate toward home-grown brands, it will undoubtedly put pressure on international brands to develop designs, features, and pricing strategies tailored to the tastes of Chinese consumers to retain their market share, as well as increase their marketing spend across all media in China, but especially digital.

It's already happening in the personal computer market, where Lenovo—a Chinese company—has leveraged its success at home to become a dominant brand on the global stage. This has, in turn, created even more of a halo at home, especially with upmarket consumers. Because Lenovo is a Chinese company, its intuitive and highly nuanced understanding of the Chinese mind-set is not surprising. But it's still instructive.

The giant personal computer, tablet, and phone maker is a prime example of successfully blending the best Chinese and Western marketing practices in order to succeed with Chinese consumers—by shaping its products, messaging, omni channel marketing approach, and CRM to identify, inspire, and engage customers across the income spectrum. By doing this across market clusters and geography, and by offering a wide range of products and multiple price points, Lenovo has leveraged the super-consumer boom to become a global player in consumer technology. Another key to their success has been their early approach to the China Global Demographic and their ability to reach Chinese consumers in the United States, Europe, and elsewhere in addition to the "China Market."

With headquarters in Beijing and in the heart of the Research Triangle in Morrisville, North Carolina—and with a research center in Singapore—Lenovo has risen to the top of the personal computer heap in a relatively short period of time.

Liu Chuanzhi founded Lenovo in Beijing in 1984—it was originally called Legend—and was incorporated in Hong Kong in 1988. After an initial attempt to import televisions failed, the company started to conduct quality-control checks for PC buyers. The breakthrough, which would set the company on the path to becoming a computer manufacturer, was its development of a circuit board for IBM-compatible PCs so they could process Chinese characters.

The company became publicly listed in Hong Kong in 1994, raising $30 million in capital. A second listing of 50 million shares, in 2000, raised an additional $200 million. Lenovo earned a reputation for producing high-quality computer products, for being well managed, and for comprehensive, transparent reporting and compliance. By 2004, Lenovo was the top producer of computers in China.

In 2005, Lenovo surprised the business and technology worlds when it purchased IBM's personal computer division for $1.25 billion and $500 million in assumed debt. Investors, financial pros, and consumers alike were left scratching their heads. "Who and what is a Lenovo?" they asked. "How did a Chinese company succeed in buying arguably one of the most important and venerable names in computing?" "What does this deal tell us about the rise of China?"

Almost overnight, the IBM deal gave Lenovo global credibility, access to numerous foreign markets, and ownership of IBM's flagship product, the ThinkPad. (Not to mention IBM's marketing, sales, technology, and best practices.)

Liu Chuanzhi noted not long after the deal that his company benefited in three ways from the IBM acquisition. "We got the ThinkPad brand, IBM's more advanced PC manufacturing technology, and the company's international resources, such as its global sales channels and operation teams. These three elements have shored up our sales revenue in the past several years."

We spoke at length with Brion Tingler, Lenovo's director of global media, about the impact of China's super consumers on the company's success.

"Our approach in China is to appeal to two markets—mature and emerging, with many levels in both camps—very differently," Tingler says. "For instance, we're branding for the mature technology consumer market as an international brand. The logo is in English, the tag line is in English, or with some translation. In the mature markets, we are competing against Apple and Samsung and trend toward higher price points. We are positioned as a global brand.

"In emerging rural, small city, and village markets, we focus heavily on distribution and channel development. Our logos, ads, and collateral are almost exclusively in Chinese and we are positioned as a Chinese company. The branding and pitch are more focused on product benefits, value, and reliability, whereas the pitch in the mature markets is more focused on the emotional, the brand connection, and customer relationships."

Tingler notes, however, that since 2009 the branding and messaging have become more unified—but significant differences in approach remain between developed and developing China.

Lenovo has followed a unique path among Chinese consumer product brands and companies. It started as an early experiment under the government's new attitude of experimentation with and tolerance for private business ownership, raised capital through a public listing, and then became a dominant domestic brand. With the IBM PC purchase it built a global brand and returned to China as a hometown hero.

Having accomplished all of this, the company reset its thinking on operations and sales in China as well as globally. Lenovo incrementally extended its product offerings, segmented its marketing and services, and successfully integrated best practices from the United States, China, and Singapore so that it could become a dominant player across categories in China and a global force to be reckoned with.

An example of the brand unification and the shift in positioning the company is the 2014 launch of its new tablet, the Yoga 2. The high-end tablet is a cutting-edge piece of technology with a breakthrough 18-hour battery life, tablet and laptop features, and a super-resolution screen. The company hired Ashton Kutcher, the American TV and movie star, as not only a celebrity endorser but as a product engineer. Kutcher is an accomplished investor, social-media pioneer, and technologist.

The product launched with a glitzy event in Los Angeles where Kutcher shared the stage with the Lenovo CEO. When the event ended, they immediately flew to Beijing and launched the product with another high-profile event. Cutting-edge technology, Western-style hype and pomp, massive media coverage, and celebrity involvement all helped further establish Lenovo as a global brand in the minds of Chinese consumers.

A large part of the success that Lenovo has had in selling higher-end technology products in China is the fact that consumers, by way of the aforementioned approach to marketing, feel good about using their Lenovo tablets or phones at the same table as their friends using iPads and Samsung G4s—they feel and believe that Lenovo products have the same cachet and appeal as the other leading products and brands.

Tingler adds that, "while success has come through great products, marketing, value, and reliability, Lenovo's growth is also because mature-market Chinese consumers are becoming a bit more like Western consumers."

"They are sophisticated, discerning, brand conscious, and young," Tingler says. "We are marketing heavily to 18- to 24-year-olds in China and abroad because they have the spending power, influence, and future potential to be lifelong Lenovo loyalists."

In other words Lenovo is changing the perception of what a Chinese technology brand is and China's mature consumer market is dictating what Lenovo needs to be. But Lenovo's success with the mature market is only half the story. Its understanding of the culture, needs, mindsets, demographics, purchasing power, and tastes of emerging China consumers—rural buyers in particular—is the foundation for the other half of the story.

"Distribution and channel dominance are keys to success in the developing and rural areas of China. But equally important is understanding the needs, price sensitivity, and service needs," Tingler notes. "We already have 20,000 outlets in China and our stated goal is to have a Lenovo touch point within 50 miles of every village and town in China. Many of our emerging-market customers are making their first PC, tablet, or phone purchase. For them guidance, support, and service are paramount."

One of they great marketing coups of the Super Consumer era was Lenovo's "Red Computer." They produced a large, almost throwback PC specifically for the rural market and more specifically for the "first computer/wedding market."

The company's commitment to research, to local insight and to ALL of China's consumers paid off. Lenovo found that first-time computer users in rural areas liked to show of their computer as a piece of furniture, not a super-thin notebook hidden under a piece of paper on the desk. They also realized there was great face for both the givers and receivers of a "wedding" PC. The resulting product was a big PC, in a big red and gold box (wedding colors) that was marketed to brides, grooms, friends, and family who would not only give one as a gift but who would want their own as well. It was a best seller. Marketing, branding, service, CRM, and open-mindedness resulted in Lenovo winning the opening battle in the fight for the rural computer user.

"Our network of stores and service centers, as well as customer support, are competitive advantages for Lenovo."

Tingler's claims ring true. Our research in the category shows that these consumers will not buy Dell or Hewlett-Packard computers because there is no local retail outlet—or very small ones where they do exist—little to no maintenance, parts, or repair services; and there is very little impact through marketing.

Lenovo understood before most companies that the Chinese super consumer lives in villages as well as Shanghai high-rises. He or she only needed to be listened to, understood, communicated with, and serviced in his or her own way.

What of the future? Lenovo knows that the number of PCs sold in the mature China markets will tail off in the coming years, but its push to dominance in tablets, phones, and other products more than makes up for that loss. Conversely, new computer buyers will fuel exponential growth in PCs and laptops in the emerging Chinese markets.

Chinese consumers are fueling the growth of Lenovo. The brand is ubiquitous in China and is gaining visibility around the world. The power of the Chinese super consumer is shaping Lenovo, and Lenovo's approach to marketing is shaping China's consumers and the consumer technology market in China.

From East to West to Wei East

Just as Lenovo parlayed its eastern/Western cachet in order to appeal to mature-market Chinese consumers, a woman from Wuhan, the steamy and spicy provincial capital of Hubei province in central China, did the same thing on her way to building a dominant brand in skincare. If you don't know the name Wei Brian or her brand, Wei East, that means you haven't watched much of the second-largest home shopping channel in America, Home Shopping Network (HSN). Wei is a celebrity host and seller of skincare products for the largest traditional Chinese medicine–based skincare line in the United States.

Millions of women have relied on Wei East's knowledge of the power of Chinese herbs to help maintain their skin's vitality and youthful appearance since 2005, and Wei's record sale of more than 1 million dollars' worth of products within 20 minutes remains unbroken.

Since she turned nine years old, Wei has been fascinated with Chinese herbs and their healing power. At her mother's side, she looked on and learned—rapt with interest—observing nature's ability to cure common human ailments. With natural treatments and beauty secrets that have been passed down from mother to daughter for more than 4,000 years, people everywhere have come to rely on the medicinal values of natural eastern remedies.

Wei continued to study herbal medicine into adulthood under the tutelage of two of China's most renowned and respected doctors. Then she went to America to pursue her degree in engineering, a popular subject among Chinese students, but quickly found that her interest didn't really lie in engineering,and she decided to pursue something she loved—beauty—and combined it with her knowledge of Chinese and Western science. Collaborating with a number of top chemists, she created the Wei East family of products.

Like some other Chinese-American immigrants, Wei has a strong accent. She also had no media training, and many HSN executives were skeptical that she would be able to go on TV and convince Americans to purchase skincare products with funny-sounding Chinese herbal ingredients such as red peony root, Tibetan chrysanthemum, Reishi mushroom, and pomegranate peel. But her passion and authenticity came through on the screen.

"Like most Chinese people, I believe in faith and I remember telling my Chinese friends when I was in China that I saw myself selling on TV in America," Wei recalls. "My friends would question me, 'Why would the Americans believe you?' and I simply said 'I don't know.'"

Wei told us that when she was young, her father shared with her a story that stuck in her mind.

"He told me there was a very famous Chinese General named Chen Yi and he loved writing poems," she recalls. "So when he was in front of his poet friends, he would always tell them 'I am a General.' However, when he was with his military friends, he would always tell them 'I am a poet.'"

When Wei first started selling beauty products in America, China had not yet reached economic prominence and most Americans still thought beauty and skincare products came exclusively from Paris or elsewhere in Europe, not from China. But Wei knew Chinese herbs and her unique value proposition resonated with an American audience.

In a short time, Wei East became one of the best-selling skincare products on the HSN network.

It was Wei's American chemist who insisted that she go on TV instead of an American spokesperson. Wei recalls her saying, "You are the real deal, you know everything about the products, and you should go on and sell."

Wei's accent—initially thought to be a liability—gave her credibility and brought the orders rushing in. She asked her audience, "What makes you buy my products? Is it what I said about the products?" The audience told her that it was not the product knowledge, but the way she communicated it. She spoke from her heart and with authenticity, and even though the viewers might not have always understood the words she tried to articulate, they understood what she meant.

Wei East's sales volume eventually reached $30 million per year. Most people would be satisfied with that. But Wei saw opportunities to introduce Chinese herbs beyond HSN, so she created another luxury line of products called Wei Beauty and started to sell those in spa product chain stores, such as SpaceNK, Hong Kong's Joyce Beauty, and Sephora in North America.

However, Wei never forgot what her father told her years ago: "You must do something for China and help Chinese women become more beautiful."

China had fast become the world's biggest market for top skincare and cosmetic brands, such as Lancôme, L'Oréal, and Estée Lauder, and Wei sensed the timing was perfect for her to go back. The Chinese business woman has become a powerhouse demographic in her own right. In *Fortune's* latest list of the 50 Most Powerful Women, Dong Mingzhu, chair and president of GREE Electric Appliances, is ranked 42nd. She joined the company as a salesperson in 1990 and helped grow the air-conditioning maker into a $16 billion worldwide appliance leader. At 49, you have Zhang Xin, CEO of Soho China, who in 2013 became co-owner of Manhattan's GM building, once the world's most expensive commercial building. During the next 10 years, successful Chinese women are likely to spend a lot more money on beauty and skincare products. According to research conducted by the Boston Consulting Group, Chinese women's earnings will grow from $1.3 trillion in 2010 to $4 trillion by 2020, up from $680 million in 2005 and $350 million in 2000. That is more than a tenfold increase in 20 years.

Moreover, seven of the 13 richest women in the world are Chinese, and four of the wealthiest are younger than 50. Since Wei was a pioneer in TV sales, she was able to negotiate a deal to pitch her products on Hunan TV, currently China's second-most-watched channel. And in less than a year, Wei has generated the total revenue volume that it took her 10 years to amass in America. Remember what we said about China years being like dog years?

She still lives in Philadelphia and goes to China three times a year to appear on television. The rest of the time, she sells through a surrogate. Born in China, Wei went to America to realize her American Dream. Now she goes back to China to realize her Chinese Dream. Like Lenovo, Wei went from East to West, and now Wei East again.

Baby Boom

Paul Zhao is one of the most hardworking, smartest, and luckiest businessmen in China today. He has worked hard at every job he has ever had, and was smart enough to turn hard work, opportunity, and experience into one of China's fastest growing consumer brands, and he is lucky because the Chinese government recently made a major decision on social policy that could double or triple his business in the next few years.

Zhao is the founder and CEO of O.C.T. Mami, the largest retailer and brand of maternity wear in China. The company has more than 900 retail outlets and 1,600 points of sale across China and has become the most popular brand and retailer in its category.

This success was by no means a sure thing when Zhao and his wife, Wenhong, founded the company in 1997.

In fact the maternity-wear category in China was virtually nonexistent then. Zhao created the category and then brilliantly built a company that would dominate it.

Paul Zhao is 45 years old and graduated from Nanjing University in 1991. He started work at a state-owned company, the East China Design and Energy Company for the Environment. Like so many of China's successful businesspeople, he studied and worked as an engineer. He concentrated on how to improve China's environment by designing earth-friendly water machinery. After 18 months he realized his passion and future were not in environmental engineering. He sought out a new opportunity and in short order found one.

He was hired by a Taiwanese specialty apparel maker to help them with their operations in Mainland China. In 1993, most of the foreign-run companies in China were either invested by or owned by companies from Greater China, including Taiwan and Hong Kong. Many Chinese entrepreneurs got their starts with such companies and were able to trade their knowledge of the mainland for experience in how to start and run a factory. Zhao was typical in this way.

The company specialized in uniforms and apparel for overseas institutional buyers, such as fire departments, police forces, military, hospitals, and others.

Also typical of this period was the second wave of foreign buyers, beyond the big multinationals, who came to China in ever-increasing numbers to source and make their goods, especially in toys, home wares, and apparel.

Zhao gained immense experience in how to operate and manage an apparel factory. The job also afforded him the opportunity to travel overseas, to Europe, the Middle East, and elsewhere. This was a time when it was still very difficult for anyone to travel for business outside of China. With rare exceptions, the only citizens allowed to leave China were officials, select businesspeople, and students.

This opportunity gave Zhao another advantage. He was able to observe and learn firsthand how foreign companies operated their businesses at all levels, how they distributed and sold their goods, and, most importantly, how they marketed their goods.

The forces of globalization and the affirmation that China's Reform and Opening movement was permanent created an opportunity for an ambitious and educated man to build something from the ground up.

Zhao's next move was to get into a partnership with a company that made bras for export. This was his entry into the world of women's wear. After learning how to make, move, market, and sell apparel—and with the dream of starting his own business—Zhao moved to Hangzhou, the beautiful city next to the West Lake on China's east coast, about three hours drive south of Shanghai in Zhejiang Province.

Zhao saw that competition was intense in the women's and men's apparel markets for export. He also saw that it was largely a low-price, low-value-add, low-margin business and wanted to find an unexploited niche. His experience in the bra business led to his idea that there was a future in maternity wear in China—a business he felt he knew well and that would provide high margins.

He discovered that, in 1996, there was only one Taiwanese company in China that produced maternity wear for export, and no company of note making it for domestic consumption. Zhao was convinced that this was his ideal niche. He began a factory that made maternity clothes for export, but his real goal all along was to create a domestic brand for China.

In 1997 O.C.T. Mami was founded. The name, somewhat unwieldy in English, was derived in a typically Chinese way. In China a pregnancy is considered to be ten months. October is the tenth month of the year, thus, O.C.T. Mami.

The company produced high-quality products made of excellent materials, and importantly, produced original designs. They found almost immediate success with exports. Flush with success, cash, and the artist's zeal to create, Zhao put his plan for a local brand into motion. It would be a brand that would feature colorful, modern, and fashionable maternity wear for China, the most populous and baby-producing nation on Earth.

Chinese women were becoming ever more fashion conscious by 2000. The middle class was growing and a wealthy class of entrepreneurs, merchants, factory owners, and businesspeople of all stripes became well established.

The second wave of Chinese consumers with disposable income was being born. By no means at this time was there anything resembling a large and sophisticated consumer class in China, never mind a super consumer. But there was enough of a consumer class looking for a more Western look and lifestyle that opportunities were presenting themselves for people like Paul Zhao and businesses like O.C.T. Mami.

The big problem, though, was that there was no market or desire for maternity wear in China at the time. Undeterred, Zhao opened the first O.C.T. Mami store in Hangzhou in 1997. He chose Hangzhou because it was a center of production for fashion, because it was a high-octane commercial city, and because it was one of China's earliest centers of consumerism.

He also wanted to keep production and retail in close proximity, so that he could react to feedback and changes in taste quickly and move product from design, to factory floor, to store shelf in weeks rather than months. The store was an almost immediate hit. Within five months a second location opened and it also succeeded.

The company concentrated on designs that were modeled on Western ones but tailored to local tastes. They also ensured that cuts and sizes were specific to the sizes and shapes of Chinese women and perhaps most importantly of all, they aggressively and smartly marketed the brand. Zhao knew that in China, brand is everything. The brand spoke to the aspiration of middle-class living and appreciation for the finer things in life. The stores were small, personal, and were soaked in the O.C.T. Mami-brand message.

Zhao relates a story about how patience, understanding the culture, and indulgence played a part in the first store's success. "At first women were bringing their tailors in and having them copy the designs on display. The tailors were charging the women about 100 RMB for custom wear. We saw this happening and allowed it. The tailors could not produce the garments correctly. We were charging 150 RMB and the garment was perfect. Slowly we convinced them that we were the experts in maternity wear and we could make them look great at a great price. This was a huge step forward for us."

Another key insight that Zhao and his team had was that, as we have covered previously, China is not one monolithic market; rather, it is a cluster of markets differentiated by custom, culture, climate, body size, and so on. He adjusted his marketing and product mix to match the markets.

Zhao's next move was to start distributing the brand in department stores. "In China every city has different department stores and distribution channels, unlike the few very big retailers in the United States. We had to work very hard to build relationships with all of them to get our products placed in this key sales channel," said Zhao.

Everywhere Zhao went, though, he was asked to provide *hongbao*, or under-the-table payments to get the brand in the stores. Zhao wanted to play it clean and refused. This made growth difficult. So from 2004 to 2005 he got his MBA with a concentration in marketing, and in 2006 he made branding and marketing the key drivers of company growth.

He engaged a major Taiwanese advertising agency and started running commercials on CCTV. By this time cash flow was faltering and so Zhao was taking a big risk by advertising on TV. This also led Zhao to seek out innovative ways to market and advertise the brand.

O.C.T. Mami was an early adopter in utilizing social media and digital advertising.

The company was also an early entrant into the still nascent e-commerce market in 2007 to 2008. By 2012 the company was not only one of the most sophisticated users of digital advertising and commerce in China, but also could be considered one of the most sophisticated in the world. The company installed full-body, digital magic mirrors that allowed mommies-to-be to see how everything the store sells would look on them. The mirrors digitally map the customer's body and then, with the wave of a hand, she can scroll through all the sizes and styles.

The company also put a feature on their website that allows you to upload your picture and then pick a celebrity picture. After clicking enter, the program creates an image of what a baby produced by the user and the celebrity would look like.

Also, in a nod to the importance of educating consumers to build markets and market share, O.C.T. Mami started an online class for new mothers that could be taken on their website. They also employed a series of celebrity spokespeople, which is perhaps even more effective and important in China than in other markets.

The company showed a willingness to learn from and spend money on a Western scale for an integrated-marketing approach. The combination of understanding the culture, language, mind-set, educational needs, and purchase motivators, combined with the smart use of technology and Western-style marketing, has made O.C.T. Miami a category giant.

The company showed such sophistication and growth that Sequoia Capital, the venerable and hugely successful California venture capital firm, invested in the company in 2011, further boosting its long-term prospects.

When we introduced Paul Zhao, we mentioned he was one of the smartest, most hard working, and luckiest businessmen in China. I think we have clearly demonstrated his smarts and hard work, but lucky? Is there any other business owner in China today you would rather be than the owner of the country's leading maternity wear company when, in January 2014, the Chinese government rescinded its one-child policy? For the first time in 30 years Chinese couples can have two or three babies—a traditional Chinese family unit.

Yes, in China luck and government policy change fast and are integral to success as much as good research, smarts, and hard work.

Brand Advertising in China

Brand advertising in China—whether in television, print, billboards, or any other mass media—has fundamental differences from the equivalent we see in the West.

Scott Markman explains, "Western brands are built on a foundation of strategy that creates differentiation and a deep embed in the memory of the consumer, while at the same time communicating a value proposition with benefits. Positioning is key, as are innovation and originality, in selling to targeted consumer segments oversaturated with options."

He continues: "Brands leverage emotional insights into those specific target segments: 'How will this product make me feel?' 'Does it address a need or want I can't get elsewhere?' 'Does it validate my self-image?' To address these desires, brand advertising uses images and words grounded in ideas that speak to the mind as well as the heart. And, for many brands, they may have segments that don't conveniently overlap, so figuring out a unified brand strategy can be challenging."

Successful Western brands understand that once they win the heart of the consumer, the consumer will reward the brand with loyalty and may stay with it for years. It's the reason that the concept of lifetime customer value drives many Western marketers' decision making.

We asked Markman how this differs in China and he said, "In China, the art and science of market segmentation takes a back seat to chasing a gigantic overall market. This isn't to say that Chinese brands don't understand to whom they are selling, but rather that the products and the ads that promote them are developed with a mind-set of 'I have a great product to sell. How big is our opportunity?' and 'How many eyeballs can I get in front of?'"

In the West the creative for brand advertising mostly revolves around the individual's values. When it comes to developing creative for products in China, though, the fundamental motivation for brands is to attach *cultural* values—such as harmony and happiness—to the brand, while signaling that the brand meets Western standards of quality and prestige. The message is this: The product is culturally copacetic and will also let you lead the life you desire.

Markman also says that "in China we produce ads in all mediums, featuring a lot of glitzy surface veneer, but very few 'big ideas' because the underlying assumption by Chinese consumers is if the TV spot's production values are shiny and sparkly, and the brand is famous, then the product must be good."

Chinese ads often contain bright colors, lots of animation and glitz, and smiling models leading a trendy life. But usually there is very little copy. Furthermore, the spots are often seen in elevator banks and big public venues with no sound so, naturally, image rules and the goal is to mesmerize the viewer.

This approach is similar with both Chinese and Western brands, whose ads are prepared by the China offices of global agencies with creative that is perhaps more idea driven, but still follows the model that works in the local market.

Going Native—Tory Burch, *Gossip Girl*, and Made-for-China TV

The growth of broadcast media has also created opportunities for brands that understand the Chinese mind-set and then form relationships with consumers. Larry Namer, the Hollywood producer who founded E! Entertainment Television, has been a driving force in this media explosion.

Namer and veteran TV executive Larry Pompadur founded Metan Development in 2009. Metan is a US company, led by American executives and staffed by Chinese nationals, that produces original programming for China.

"I was amazed at how much younger the people with money were in China. The average Chanel buyer there is 20 years younger than in the West," says Mr. Namer. "These are young people who watch Western shows and buy Western products, and increasingly watch their TV on the Internet. We saw an opportunity to put that all together."

All of the company's employees—in China and the United States—are native Chinese who attended radio, TV, and film programs at American universities. For production and filming, Metan partners with Meitian Me You, a Chinese production company.

Metan has been a boon for brands and products associated with its shows. Advertising, in particular, is expensive, highly fragmented, and hard to measure in China. There are more than 2,000 TV stations in China and it has one of the largest newspaper industries in the world, a fast-growing movie industry, and is now home to nearly 600 million

Internet users who chat, blog, shop, argue, and watch TV shows and movies on millions of websites. Younger generations of Chinese have shifted their TV and movie-viewing habits online in record numbers.

"There are about 400 million people who now watch TV on the Internet in China, mostly on their laptops, and there are more than 100 Western TV shows licensed by giant video sites like Youku Tudou that are very popular," Namer says.

Increasingly those shows are impacting the products that Chinese consumers choose to buy. One example is Tory Burch. When Chinese women went online and started to watch *Gossip Girl* (the New York–based show that followed the fortunes of four wealthy young women), they saw the characters wearing Tory Burch handbags. Almost overnight, Tory Burch bags became a must-have item for young adults in China. Everyone was talking about the brand and sales spiked. Tory Burch officially entered China in 2011, two years after their bags became a cultural icon.

This, and other similar examples, demonstrate the impact of popular culture as a brand builder and purchase motivator in China. Seeing the growth of Internet TV viewing, in addition to the billion people who watch broadcast TV (and the impact that quality programs could have for brands featured on the right shows), Metan set out to create original programming for Chinese audiences—programming that would meld the love of Western shows and high-production values with content that was of, by, and for China.

Metan's first hit—and still one of its most popular Internet and TV shows—is *Hello Hollywood!* The show is a mix of gossip, news, and entertainment and is full of glamorous images of celebrities, California living, and the brands and retailers that clothe, feed, house, and entertain the Hollywood elite. It airs on 45 stations in China and six in the United States, and it averages more than 10 million viewers. An additional 11 million view it on the Internet.

From this success, the company began production of original TV series for the Internet. The first was *Planet Homebuddies* (now called *Modern Life*), a sitcom about young, urban, white-collar workers who live at home, which is common in China. It went live on the four biggest web portals (Youku Tudou, iQiyi, PPTV, and Sina), ranking seventh on Tudou, with a record 3 million viewers in the first week after the first episode was released.

Then came *Return to Da Fu Tsun*, a comedy-drama series developed by Namer. After finding early success in Beijing and selling his company, a father decides to move his family back to the rural village of Da Fu Tsun (大福村) in order to relearn the meaning of family values and community. The series is shown online and on CCTV-8 and attracts a combined 14 million viewers. To put these viewer numbers in perspective, popular cable shows in the United States attract 2 to 5 million viewers per week. The series finale of *Breaking Bad* drew 10.3 million.

Metan's business model is simple and effective. In the case of shows for broadcast TV, the stations buy the shows and then sell advertising around them. In the case of Internet shows, the portals pay Metan to license the show. Then, both sides sell advertising around it. Both models utilize product integration—the insertion of products, brands, and retailers into the show.

There are three levels at which a brand can participate:

1. The product is featured in the background or foreground.
2. The product is used by the characters.
3. The product is essential to the plot and can drive an episode or a season.

Usually Metan gets the first anchor brand or product in. After that, it licenses the show and both companies seek other brands and products for integration. Competition for shows has grown fierce between rival portals and most demand exclusivity. This increases the value of quality shows. Additionally, pirate sites are on the decline because the portals are paying large sums for content and have convinced the government to crack down.

Bacardi, Lavazza Coffee, and Lee Jeans have all been placed on *Planet Homebuddies*, with noticeable results. In fact, Bacardi was actually a plot driver. One of the main characters wanted to become a bartender and live the high life in Shanghai, so he attended an eight-week course at the Bacardi School of Bartending.

Namer has created a win–win–win situation for all involved. The audience gets the kind of content it loves; the stations and portals get big traffic and great revenues; brands reach target audiences with measurable effects on brand awareness, popularity, and sales.

Metan Development makes money doing what it does best: creating engaging and relevant entertainment that is both popular and profitable.

The Role of Social Media in Marketing: United States versus China

In recent years, marketing trends in the United States have shifted dramatically toward social media and away from traditional forms of media such as broadcast, print, and outdoors. The twin dynamics of information sharing and direct consumer response to brands (even author content) have enabled American consumers to become active participants in their relationships to the brands they admire.

This has created a permanent change in the approach that marketers take in serving the needs of consumers. Brands can no longer merely talk at consumers, interrupting their lives in a one-way transmission of persuasive arguments. They need to approach marketing communications as a running dialogue, where they must listen as much as they speak. They must also be mindful of the influence that a single consumer has on many others, through reviews and comments.

But how did the idea of social media as a communications platform develop? What were the cultural assumptions that led to the creation of blogging software, social-networking sites, photo-sharing sites, political-action sites (such as change.org), and so on?

Most likely, it was rooted in the American ideals of individualism, self-expression, and freedom of speech. As Americans, we love to find a soapbox to stand on and voice our opinion. We're also brought up in an educational system built upon the Socratic exchange of ideas and the questioning of authority. Our values celebrate this way of thinking, and we find outlets for it in all walks of life. It remains the foundation for innovation and for our entrepreneurial spirit.

That being the case, is the construct upon which social media happens similar in China—where politics are authoritarian, information is controlled, individualism not as prominent, and the cultural framework is oriented towards the masses?

The answer is yes and no.

Prior to the advent of social media in China, there was little, if any, opportunity for self-expression among everyday citizens. For many, this was akin to learning how to ride a bike, and once they got the hang of 140-character bursts of commentary, they discovered they liked it. And so, Sina Weibo (a hybrid of Twitter and Facebook) became a raging success, helped by official prohibition of Twitter and Facebook in China.

But like all media in China it is closely monitored, and there are topics that are censored or blocked. Now comes WeChat, a cell phone application developed by Tencent in China and first released in January 2011. Like WhatsApp and Instagram, its primary purpose is to enable easy information and life-moment sharing with friends and fans through the user's mobile phone. It also has become a raging success, with 600 million registered users in China and around the world (mostly Chinese living abroad).

Not surprisingly, as WeChat usage has soared, so has Weibo usage correspondingly declined. And, as WeChat has smartly added a range of features and functionality, it seems as though many Chinese prefer using social-media tools to serve more personal, gratifying purposes, such as:

- Connecting with friends and sharing information.
- Accomplishing more and centralizing tasks.
- Participating in trendy activities.
- Showing support for the brands they favor.
- Paying for products.

THE POWER OF WECHAT

So how do you engage Chinese super consumers if you are in New York and not in Beijing?

Obviously if you are a large luxury retailer like Louis Vuitton or Chanel, the answer is simple—just open a flagship store on Fifth Avenue and on Hua Hai Lu and they will come to you. But what if you're a professional who sells a professional service?

In March 2014, Emma Hao discovered China's popular social media and messaging app, WeChat, and she gained notoriety closing two real estate transactions valued at more than $13 million using the app.

Unlike most WeChat users, who use the service to swap messages, post pictures, and share personal updates, Emma Hao—a Manhattan-based agent at the global real-estate brokerage Douglas Elliman—received an unsolicited message on WeChat from a Chinese chairman, who wanted to know more about a luxury residential building in Manhattan called Baccarat Residence, which was designed by the well-known architect Tony Ingrao. Hao left a message with the Chinese entrepreneur on WeChat, and after visiting the Baccarat sales center, she sent her pictures of the condo's luxurious amenities. The next day, after speaking with the woman by phone, Hao closed two deals: a $10.25 million three-bedroom apartment on the thirty-ninth floor and a one-bedroom unit on the twenty-first floor for approximately $3 million.

It seemed like a stroke of luck to do $13 million in transactions on a Chinese social media tool, but the real story — like most other success stories — requires a little more explanation.

Born in Beijing, Emma Hao worked as a journalist in the Ministry of Construction and got a B.A. in Chinese literature. She then went to the University of Brighton in the U.K., got her MBA, and immigrated to the United States. Seeing the number of Chinese people traveling, working, studying, and buying property abroad, she entered the real estate business.

In the beginning it was challenging, but Emma started to rent apartments to Chinese students who were studying at New York University, Pace University, or Columbia. These students did not have much of a budget and they could only afford apartments in the range of $600 to $800 per month. Knowing that it would be impractical to find any apartments in the price range, Emma tried to look for creative solutions to serve these clients. She eventually found apartments on Roosevelt Island — a small island connected to Manhattan by a cable-car service — that offered big promotions for its apartments in order to attract tenants to this newly developed area.

"I was probably one of the first Chinese real estate agents to discover Roosevelt Island as they were giving away three months of free rent and a free Metro Card (the card for New York City subway riders) if you signed a one-year lease," Hao says. "I was taking 30 to 40 Chinese students with me to Roosevelt Island to help them find inexpensive apartments close to Manhattan and their schools."

Besides helping the students find apartments, Emma helped many open bank accounts, since some spoke little English. This laid the foundation for relationships with these students, who were often the sole children of wealthy Chinese super consumers. Emma also uses WeChat to communicate with their parents and explain to them what she is doing to help their children.

This is a useful lesson. You can build trusting relationships with Chinese super consumers by helping their children. In other words: Do good to do well.

One of WeChat's unique features is the hold-and-talk function, which works like a walkie-talkie. Hao has used it, combined with her excellent writing skills, to produce a daily WeChat journal with pictures. She also writes about the differences between short-term rental targets and long-term investments.

(continued)

(*continued*)

Finally, Hao has made it a practice to take selfies in front of apartment mirrors in order to ensure that people know she's actually been inside the apartment.

Chinese students have started to bring more parents into Hao's WeChat group, and some parents feel as though they've become personal friends with Hao. As we've explained, relationships are the most valuable currency when marketing to Chinese super consumers.

The real estate purchasing process is dramatically different in China, so Hao has further differentiated herself from other real estate agents by setting up dedicated WeChat groups that include herself, the buyer, and attorneys in order to help navigate the purchasing process.

"I help them make their documents match the requirements of the condo board," Hao says. "For example, when buying an apartment in China, they won't need your W2 tax return so most Chinese do not even know how to prove their income. I would suggest to them to talk to their human resources departments and issue a letter stating their income as a proof of income.

"I also explain to the Chinese buyers that the lengthy process of board approval is designed to protect you and other tenants."

For the past two years, Emma estimates she's completed seven real estate transactions via the app.

"No matter how prospective Chinese clients first contacted me, we almost always end up using WeChat at some point," she says. "Chinese today have a lot of cash and they like to buy real estate with that cash, without borrowing. Once they trust you, they will give you all their referrals since we have become friends. [Building trust] takes a longer time than with other groups, but they don't shop around anymore. My American buyers continue to shop around even after we did business."

So what to make of these broad trends and their implications for Chinese consumer behavior? Probably that it's safer, more comfortable, and pleasurable for Chinese to participate in a way that aligns with Chinese societal values and stays within safe boundaries. In a very simplistic view, WeChat is functional and happy; Weibo is open-ended but flirts with trouble.

The big takeaway for marketers regarding social media in China is that it again comes back to history and culture. More than any other culture in the world, Chinese people make purchasing decisions based on peer input and recommendations from trusting friends and family. Social media has developed into the most important marketing channel in China because it provides the platform for peer recommendations, relationship building, and personal expression in an environment where expression is limited.

Promotions

Coupon design and loyalty programs are much more sophisticated in China than in the United States.

Dr. Baohong Sun, a professor of marketing at the prestigious Cheung Kong Graduate School of Business (CKSB), notes that there are 10 ways to offer and promote coupons in China, including loyalty points, coupons for alternate products, coupons for sister businesses, or coupons for something for free. She notes that no matter the media, promotions are very effective, to a point.

"In Chinese society everything is subject to negotiation, so promotions allow for ongoing negotiation of price and value," said Dr. Sun.

But there is a limit. Overpromotion can weaken a brand. Chinese consumers are always looking for information and clues about a brand's quality, and price is a key signal. If a brand offers too many discounts it will revise the consumer's impression of the brand's quality downward.

Dr. Sun adds, "You also need to be careful about what kind of products you offer promotions on. Fast-moving consumer products, like toilet paper, don't need promotions. But specialty products, where a brand is trying to build acceptance and market share—say strawberries and yogurt—can benefit from promotions."

Another downside: If the proper balance is not found, the promotion will produce a spike in sales in the short term, but there will be a prolonged dip afterwards because consumers may delay the next purchase as they wait for the next promotion. Offering many types of promotions can mitigate this, not just deep discounts.

In review some keys to marketing in China include:

- The China media landscape is huge—therefore it is crucial to understand the strengths and weaknesses of each channel and to focus your advertising on those that will provide you with the best ROI. "National" campaigns are virtually impossible.
- China's super consumers are everywhere in China and exist at all spending levels. Spending is no longer confined to the 400 million

coastal inhabitants. Tailor your products and services correctly and you can win across demographic and geographic lines.

- Peer recommendations and group acceptance are key to brand building—social media is the most important tool in your belt to build group loyalty and consensus.
- Marketing needs to be focused on a mix of the Chinese social culture dynamic along with personal aspirations. Big ideas take a back seat to promoting cultural values and individual aspirations.
- Culturally attuned marketing can help create markets for new product categories.

CHAPTER 19

The Chinese Luxury and Premium Market

C hinese consumers now account for 27 percent of all global luxury product purchases. Think about that, one out of four luxury handbags, watches, cars, jewelry, and pieces of apparel sold wind up in the hands, closets, and garages of Chinese super consumers. Luxury purchases were early drivers of the Chinese consumer boom. The first consumers in China who could afford foreign goods were the first wave of newly wealthy entrepreneurs, merchants, factory owners, and megabusiness managers—and, aside from a few fast-moving consumer goods (FMCG) companies, the first foreign retail and consumer product players in China were luxury companies.

The luxury category still is and will remain a consumer growth engine for the Chinese economy and for local and foreign brands and retailers alike.

Over the past 10 years, many European and American luxury companies have been buoyed, enriched, and, in some cases, saved by Chinese luxury consumers, especially after the crash of 2008. Companies like LVMH, Prada, and others, who saw the bottom fall out in the United States and Europe, remained profitable or became more profitable due to their China business.

While luxury consumers in China were once a very small, very wealthy, and hard-to-measure elite, luxury spending now includes a wide range of consumers across class, income, and regional lines.

It is also critical to note that while Chinese consumers account for more than one quarter of all luxury purchases globally, 60 percent of those purchases are made outside of Mainland China, including Hong Kong, Paris, New York, Los Angeles, Las Vegas, Sydney, Tokyo, London, and other global cities.

This harkens back to the importance of all (but especially luxury) companies to understand the nature and nuances of the China global demographic. Here, we will cover a few important topics regarding the luxury market and China.

1. Who are China's new luxury consumers?
2. The traits of successful luxury brands in China.
3. The myths and realities of China's luxury downturn.
4. The growth of experiential luxury.

Chinese luxury consumers can generally be categorized into three groups (with stress on *generally* because drilling down on subgroups, market characteristics, consumer demographics, and the right fit for your brand requires a lot of investment and hard work).

The Nouveau Riche: Pebble Beach or Nothing

The Chinese nouveau riche acquired their vast wealth over the past two decades. They and their families purchase luxury goods within the mainland and abroad. They were the first buyers, and have since become the most experienced, sophisticated, and well traveled of China's consumers. They include the business, technology, industrial, and political elite, and they are generally not particularly sensitive to price. The majority of China's nouveau riche reside in first- to third-tier cities.

Christine Lu is the founder and CEO of Affinity China, a specialty travel and luxury consulting and services firm, which has given her a firsthand perspective of the Chinese luxury consumer's evolution from a desire for *things* to a craving for *moments*.

"The very wealthiest and most sophisticated in China do not want to be treated like targets by brands," Lu says. "They are smart, they know if you are thinking, 'Oh, here comes a whale, let's land him.' Those days are over for this elite group. That may work with other categories of luxury buyers, but not the ultra-elite. They do not want to be treated like numbers."

Lu further explains that, "what they do want are unique prestige experiences—anyone with money can buy a $50,000 watch. They already know and buy best-of-class brands.

"They want courtside seats at basketball games, invitations to movie openings and important parties, to buy a vineyard, not just to drink wine from one."

Lu provides an anecdote that drives this point home. "We had a client who was a golf fanatic. He had a favorite golfer and a favorite golf course, Pebble Beach in California. While he built his fortune and influence in China on using relationships and social capital in relation to his talents, that social capital meant nothing in the United States."

With a few key phone calls, Lu arranged for him to play a round at Pebble Beach with his favorite PGA golfer.

"Yes, it cost him money, $75,000, but he got a singular experience that money alone could not buy and through the relationship with the golfer he was introduced to several American businesspeople who he ended up cutting deals with down the line," Lu says.

Lu makes a great point here. Yes, he took his family to California—and spent at luxury hotels, retailers, and restaurants—but the experiences and connections that he could not buy on his own were the keys to the trip.

The Gifting Group

Consumers in this group generally buy luxury goods on a mass scale within Mainland China and increasingly from abroad for gifting (mainly for business or government-related purposes). They are not always sensitive to price differences because their corporations will cover costs. And if it is purely a person-to-person gift, the impression and social capital gained are more important than the prices. That said, there is a huge demand for luxury and premium products bought in the United States and Europe that are sent or carried back to China for gifting purposes. The key market opportunity with this group is that gifting is an ingrained part of Chinese culture, and it is an important way to build and maintain relationships and networks.

China's Engine: The New Middle Class Seeks Quality and Value

By far the biggest cohorts in population and potential are the Chinese middle-class consumers, who are brand conscious but not always brand loyal, and who are price conscious but not always price sensitive. They often work and reside in first- or second-tier cities, but are increasingly hailing from third- and fourth-tier cities. These are among the newest luxury buyers and the products, price points, and designs that appeal to them are more akin to what the nouveau riche were buying five or 10 years ago. Product quality, prestige, and the appeal of badge brands are important to them.

One luxury brand that has been able to find a sweet spot in middle-class China is Brooks Brothers. The clothier's well-established positioning as a maker of reasonably affordable, but exceptionally crafted clothing is a slam dunk in a marketplace that prioritizes functionality and quality.

Three years ago, Andy Lew became managing director of Asia Pacific at Brooks Brothers. He was already living in Shanghai and working for another Italian ready-wear fashion company. With more than 200 years of history, Brooks Brothers is one of the oldest American-heritage fashion companies.

"It is inherent in the Chinese DNA to want to learn and they have an insatiable appetite for learning about products," Lew says. "The speed in which they learn what I call sophistication of fashion sense or independent fashion sense is very quick. You will see that younger people are very aggressive. They dress in what I call Japanese street fashion, and there is also the urban professional who wears suits, shirts, ties, and sport jackets."

He adds: "The evolution that I see is that they are gradually moving away from big logos. Now they have their own sense of style, mostly sensibility fashion, or a more refined fashion in a way. From the beginning, Brooks Brothers has always focused on price-value and we were never a flashy, big-logo brand like some other top luxury brands in China."

Some 40 percent of Brooks Brothers' stores are in China's first-tier cities, although every company defines first-tier differently.

"For Brooks Brothers—besides Shanghai, Beijing, and Shenzhen—Chengdu is also a first-tier city for us, because it is the window to Western China. It falls very well under China's go-west strategy," Lew says. "Shenyang and Xi'an are considered strong second-tier cities in China."

Brooks Brothers has also effectively taken advantage of its American manufacturing base in a culture that has come to associate *Made in America* with status and desirability.

"We are one of the very few brands that are still manufacturing in America," Lew says. "As an American-heritage brand, we have our suit factories in Massachusetts, tie factories in New York City and Long Island City, and our shirt factory is in North Carolina. Very, very few of our competitors can make this claim. It is very challenging because most of our competitors are sourced in Asia and China, but I know Chinese customers love to buy products made in America versus made in China."

This leads us to an important development among Chinese consumers. That is the rapid progress and importance of the affordable luxury sector. As the economy matures and growth slows somewhat, and as consumers become more interested in lifestyle than pure status symbols, affordable luxury brands are positioned for massive growth.

Affordable Luxury: A Tiffany's Tie Clip and an Entry-Level BMW

A few years ago, the concept of "affordable or accessible luxury" as a market mover in China was little more than a dot on the horizon. Today, the situation couldn't be more different. Affordable luxury brands (and traditional luxury brands that have expanded into the affordable luxury sector) have seen significant growth marked by rapid and profitable retail expansion, increased e-commerce sales, a loyal following of new middle-class customers, and renewed interest and sales from older, wealthier legacy customers.

Some brands sell only in the luxury space, never discounting and never marketing lower-priced or starter products. But other global luxury brands offer products in all three luxury categories (ultra, premium, and affordable luxury). For instance, you can buy a $40,000, $80,000 or $160,000 BMW; at Tiffany's, you can spend $80,000 on a ring, $5,000 on a necklace, or $200 on a tie clip. In many cases, luxury brands develop separate accessible luxury lines, establishing their own brand identities in the global marketplace. Emporio Armani, which earlier this year opened a watch and jewelry store in Hong Kong, is poised for a leap to the mainland.

Historically, established European labels selling premium and ultra-luxury products to well-heeled Chinese consumers have dominated the luxury segment in China. But with urban, professional income ranging from $15,000 to $100,000 per year in first- and second-tier cities like Shanghai and Suzhou, and urban per-capita disposable income around $4,000 to $6,000 per year, a large new group of middle-class consumers (some 300 million of them) are emerging who seek luxury and accessible-luxury products.

The rise of the affordable-luxury sector has coincided with, and in part been fueled by, an increasing interest in American brands such as Coach, Michael Kors, and Kate Spade, which are expanding on the mainland. American brands in other lifestyle categories are succeeding as well, and are helping blaze the trail for the apparel, footwear, and accessory sectors. But accessible luxury growth is by no means limited to US brands. H&M, Zara, and local favorite Shanghai Tang are succeeding as well.

This sector has become a key growth driver for the China luxury market, yet there is still some confusion on the part of brands and retailers about what defines accessible luxury in China, who the key consumers are, what trends are driving growth in the segment, and what strategies are working. Here is a breakdown of some of the trends as they relate to the Chinese consumer's maturation process and the emergence of the three categories of luxury: ultra, premium, and affordable luxury.

- **Been There, Done That.** There is a sophisticated cohort of wealthy legacy luxury consumers who are looking to expand their purchasing options. These consumers are open to experimenting with new brands, new styles, and expanded offerings from trusted luxury brands—even at lower price points. They want to be leaders and trendsetters, not followers, and their discoveries in the accessible-luxury sector address this interest.
- **Teach Me.** A new cohort of middle-class luxury consumers is seeking guidance on how to create a personal lifestyle. These consumers are looking to do this through a mix of accessible-luxury and luxury purchases—a $2,000 handbag, for instance, accessorized with a more modest, accessible-luxury scarf or shoes.
- **The Pioneers.** Outbound China travel has exploded over the past two years. Chinese travelers are projected to take 150 million

outbound trips by 2020, making them the world's most prolific travelers. These business and pleasure travelers—as well as students studying abroad—are exposed to brands they've never seen in China, or that have low profiles there. And when these travelers return, they seek these brands. They've known Louis Vuitton for years, but abroad they may discover such accessible luxury brands as C-Wonder or Belstaff.

- **Home Sweet Home.** A transformation from house to home/ sanctuary is fueling sales in luxury audio, furniture, artwork, décor, and upscale hardware. Accessible-luxury and luxury brands have an opportunity to seize on this newfound desire for inside as well as outside luxury. Delorme, the French bedding company, is ahead of the curve in this market, and Bang & Olufsen is making a major new investment and expansion in China. Also of note: Ralph Lauren will be opening lifestyle floors, selling home décor, within their stores in major shopping malls, such as Shanghai's Plaza 66.
- **Youth Movement.** China's young consumers are style conscious and lifestyle conscious. Those who live at home, subsidized by family, can spend upwards of 80 to 150 percent of their income on consumer products. They see accessible luxury goods as signifiers of status, indi- viduality, and lifestyle orientation. If you can sell them a $500 bag now, as family wealth increases you may well sell them a $5,000 bag a few years down the road.
- **The Red, White, and Blue.** We foresee a continually growing interest among Chinese consumers in American brands and retailers, American style, and American aspirational living. The classic Euro- pean, ultra, and luxury labels will continue to grow and prosper, but now there is room for more players at the table.

Looking at which international brands are growing and expanding in China and where the demographics are headed, there is no doubt that accessible luxury is now a key market driver in China. It is in the expansion of Coach, Michael Kors, and a dozen other American companies reporting profits from China—as well as European luxury companies offering new product levels and lifestyle stores—that we see the proof. As they experiment with their own personal brands, images, and styles, Chinese consumers want affordable luxury as well as traditional luxury and ultra-luxury products. Companies that spend the time and resources to understand the opportunity, to establish the right infrastructure—product mix, pricing models, and brand positioning—may well find that the accessible luxury sector is a driver of success in mainland markets.

China's Luxury Downturn: Myths and Realities

吃苦 (chī kǔ) means "eat bitterness." For centuries Chinese people have used this term to teach and remind themselves and their children that it is important to endure hardship, to develop a thick skin, and to keep persevering no matter how many obstacles stand in the way. Ultimately one will get through tough times and succeed. Luxury companies currently operating in China, and those considering market entry, are looking back on 2013–2014 as a period where growth in the premium luxury market slowed.

Things were especially hard for companies that depend on gifting (an important cultural and business practice in China) and for high-end restaurants and beverage purveyors.

We have preached *chi ku* as a corporate philosophy to the hundreds of companies that we have worked with on entering and growing in China over the past 12 years and we advise luxury brands to internalize it now as well. While there is an overall downturn, marked by steeper drops in some categories than others, and marked by upticks in others, the overall trajectory of the luxury industry—like that of the overall consumer market in China—still points up. So stay the course; there are still many opportunities to succeed in China. Nevertheless, here are some of the factors that have driven luxury purchase growth on the mainland down from 7 to 15 percent to about 2 percent, over the past few years.

1. President Xi Jinping is intent on making a huge dent in the endemic corruption in Chinese politics and business. Luxury items are sometimes used as a form of currency for favors and *guanxi* (reciprocal relationships). One way Beijing is enforcing its anticorruption edicts is by cracking down on gift giving, government group buying, and conspicuous consumption. The government sees luxury buying as an outcome of officials receiving *hongbao* (payoffs, bribes). All of this is causing some wealthy Chinese private citizens and public employees to think twice about buying and wearing $50,000 watches and $10,000 suits and drinking $1,000 bottles of Baiju at nightly banquets.

2. The desire for and increased sales of accessible luxury brands has been a key growth driver in China's luxury market. This trend is also fueling a desire among the nouveau riche as well as emerging middle-class luxury consumers for the casual luxury of American brands and lifestyle living. As a result, there has been an effect on the sales of top-tier luxury products, but there has also been an upside. Brands like Coach, Michael Kors, and Tory Burch are thriving in China.

3. Chinese luxury spending on the mainland is down in part because Chinese global consumer purchases are up in the rest of the world. Almost 60 percent of all luxury purchases made by Chinese citizens take place outside the mainland.

4. Chinese luxury consumers are turning increasingly toward spending their ample disposable income on lifestyle/experiential purchases in addition to pure social-status products.

Dave Gross, an expert in Chinese luxury, travel, and hospitality, also points out that "the intense competition among established and new entrants to the Chinese luxury market" has affected growth for established brands and that "the growth of e-commerce has driven prices and value down for many of the previously highly desirable brands." Online sales of brands like Gucci and Prada have increased and are not always sold through brand-sanctioned platforms.

This has made some luxury companies nervous. Some are considering slowing their China growth and others are even considering pulling out altogether. Sidelining, shrinking, or avoiding China is a huge mistake for luxury companies. This slowdown is temporary; China is and will remain the most important luxury market in the world.

Here are some key reasons for luxury brands to continue investing in China as a long-term growth market and not to make impulsive short-term decisions.

- After 30 years of exponential economic growth and development, China's economy is slowing, but this is slowing from 10 percent to 6 or 7 percent. Growth is still robust and luxury purchases will continue to increase with the economy's expansion.
- Urbanization and the ever-enlarging middle and upper classes are fueling further growth for the best things in life—while first-tier cities and regions have been saturated, the new growth will come from the

second, third, fourth, and fifth tiers, where a potential 300 million new luxury buyers reside.

- Current events and government policy are always fluid in China. When the differences between legitimate and illegitimate purchases are sorted out "this too shall pass."
- The accessible luxury market will continue to grow and prosper.

Sage Brennan, cofounder of consultancy China Luxury Advisors, and an expert in Chinese luxury branding and retail, says that "nothing has really changed, there are always ups and downs in the China market. This is a down, but the consumer is still spending; they just might not be spending where the brand is investing."

Brennan also notes that "growth opportunities over the last few years [that] have come from emerging consumers remain a deep and long lasting trend—along with overseas spending. Brands need to focus on these realities."

There are some key strategies luxury brands can implement to prosper in a temporary downturn that will also have long-term positive benefits:

- Invest in identifying, attracting, serving, and retaining the global Chinese traveler. With more than 100 million Chinese people traveling abroad in the next couple of years, and almost 60 percent of Chinese luxury purchases taking place outside the mainland, luxury brands must follow Tourneau's lead (see Chapter 13) and invest in the global and lifestyle desires and needs of Chinese luxury consumers.
- Integrate domestic, global, and China operations more closely.
- Invest in more robust e-commerce and social media strategies inside the China market.
- Rethink product lines, price points, and merchandising.
- Focus on ALL levels of luxury consumers, present and emerging.

Gross also says "brands must better manage a global inventory and sales system that understands how Chinese approach luxury purchasing. The Chinese customer is now global. The sooner those companies understand this the better. In most cases, China is a separate profit center, competing with other regions for the same customer. Thus, they do not share data across national borders."

The premium luxury market has definitely slowed, but it will pick up again soon. It may grow even faster over the next 10 years because of the established luxury–demographic cohorts and the fact that 300 to 400 million potential new buyers are coming online. Luxury brands and retailers need to continue to invest in China, but they also need to adjust their strategies for both short- and long-term growth. In other words, luxury companies must eat bitterness now and embrace the promise of a sweet dessert.

CHAPTER 20

Travel and Tourism

Certainly, travel is more than the seeing of sights; it is a change that goes on, deep and permanent, in the ideas of living.

—Mary Ritter Beard

If you are in the business of serving tourists and business travelers and you do not have a comprehensive plan in place or being executed to serve Chinese travelers, you may not be in business much longer.

Paul Biederman, a professor of travel and tourism at New York University and a former high-ranking TWA executive, provides a good introduction to the way in which China's super consumers are changing the face of global travel and hospitality: "With the largest population on earth, a rapidly expanding middle class, and relaxed government restrictions on overseas travel, it was inevitable that China would become the 800-pound gorilla in the international travel market.

"That expectation became reality in 2012 when, according to UN/WTO statistics, China became the world's leader in both numbers of outbound travelers and total overseas expenditures. Since then, China's positive margins have only widened. The United States, once the world's leader in both categories, is an ever-distant second. In 2014, China's outbound numbers and spending were expected to reach 110 million. What's so auspicious about China's volume of outbound tourism is that only 11 countries in the world have populations as large.

"Tourism represents the type of spending that comes naturally to middle-class consumers along with other components, like comfortable housing, a family, and perhaps an auto—all staples of the kind of lifestyle enjoyed in developed and developing countries alike. For China, in particular, a pent-up demand has bolstered recent travel consumption. This was fueled by the authorities only gradually withdrawing their reluctance to allow China's consumption-crazed and curious citizens to travel outside the country's boundaries. Presently, ordinary Chinese are allowed to visit 150 countries where only a relative handful of foreign destinations were accessible a decade ago."

As previously discussed in the China global demographic and luxury chapters, it is obvious that outbound travel in China is becoming ever more important to where, how, why, and on what Chinese consumers spend. But it is worth examining the impact that Chinese travelers, both outbound and within China, are having on retailers, brands, hotels, airlines, specialty-service companies, cities, states, and entire countries.

Roy Graff, an expert in Chinese travel, tourism, and the future of Chinese travel, provided us with the graph below (Figure 20.1). Like so many other aspects of China's development over the past 30 years, the rate of growth in the number of Chinese outbound travelers is almost hard to believe. There were fewer than 10 million Chinese outbound travelers in 2001. By 2010 it was more than 50 million, and in 2014 the number grew to 100 million. Within two years, we expect to see 200 million outbound Chinese travelers.

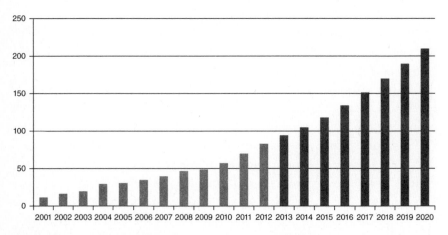

Figure 20.1   Outbound Chinese Travelers (Millions)

It's no wonder that Chinese business travelers and tourists are fast becoming the most sought after and influential in the world. Thirty years ago, travel outside of China was highly restricted, limited to structured business delegations, high-level politicians, and a few select state-owned-company executives. It wasn't until the late 1970s and early 1980s when the state began to let a small number of people to study abroad. In all three cases, the goal was to better understand how the outside world functioned and to learn how to implement Opening and Reform.

Roy Graff explains that "Outbound travel, even in modest numbers, did not begin in earnest until the mid-1990s. It is worth remembering that the handover of Hong Kong, from the U.K. back to China, did not occur until 1997 and was therefore off limits to mainlanders. In 2013, according to the Hong Kong tourism commission, there were more than 40 million arrivals from the mainland, accounting for 75 percent of all foreign arrivals to the city; 58 percent of those were one-day visits."

Hong Kong has become an important destination for mainlanders who want to buy everything from handbags, jewelry, and food, to health and beauty products. Chinese visitors also go to Hong Kong to experience a different, more Western and pan-Asian lifestyle. It is as much a holiday destination as shopping mecca.

Graff recalls how different things were even prior to the early 2000s. "When I started selling travel products and services in China in 1998 it was almost exclusively focused on business and political delegations."

Until the mid-2000s, most outbound leisure travel by Chinese took place in the form of very regimented group tours. Graff explains that most travelers had very small budgets and even less experience in travel so "they relied on big state-owned travel wholesalers or foreign travel companies who operated out of Hong Kong (it was illegal for travel agents to operate in China) who took their budget, and slotted them into a large group.

"They would typically do 10 days in Europe or the United States, quickly moving from city to city, on the bus, off the bus, on the bus, and off the bus," Graff recalls. "They stayed in cheap hotels, ate even cheaper Chinese food, and mostly took pictures at key cultural sites."

In 2002 Graff and his company began focusing on FITs (fully independent travelers), and over the past 10 years he has helped educate

Chinese travelers, travel companies, and foreign businesses on the benefits and execution of independent travel. With the growth of China's consumer boom and the birth of China's super consumers, along with government policies that allowed more independent and free travel, FITs—like the Tang family from Chapter 13—have become the norm.

Chinese travelers are poised to become the most numerous in the world by 2015 and they already spend more per capita, per trip than any other nationality—close to $7,000 per trip.

The means by which and reasons why the Chinese travel have also changed. Group tours are an ever-shrinking part of the equation. They are still important for first-time or inexperienced travelers to certain countries, but even these tours have changed. Accommodations, itineraries, and food are now higher end.

Concurrently, the trade and business delegation travel model has lost its importance. Yes, those models still exist—and yes, some of them provide useful venues for Chinese and foreign business people to interact—but, more and more, Chinese businesspeople travel on their own schedule and money, and with their own agenda.

Travel is now high on the list of ways in which Chinese people express their Chinese Dream. They want to see the world as well as learn about and interact with other cultures—to be able to spend their hard-earned money on not just goods but experiences.

Key motivators for outbound travel in 2014 include:

- **Business:** Chinese businesspeople and businesses are growing ever more confident about their place in the world, and as China Going Global accelerates (the process by which Chinese companies expand internationally in order to get publicly listed, buy land and assets, invest in new businesses, sell their brands, and buy companies), so do the number of individuals and small groups of individuals conducting business travel.
- **Shopping:** Chinese tourists and businesspeople still love to shop abroad. Prices abroad are anywhere from 30 to 60 percent lower than in China and the desire to shop and save money is still strong.
- **Lifestyle Experience:** Chinese travelers, more than ever, want to experience other cultures and lifestyles. Chinese travelers no longer exclusively stay in cheap hotels and eat cheap food so they can focus

on shopping. The hotels, the restaurants, and the cultural aspects of travel are and will continue to be big motivators.

- **Environment:** This refers to both the natural and emotional environments in China. People work very hard, long hours and have to, as one friend put it, "constantly think in six layers," adding that, "when I travel, I can think in one layer and relax." Additionally, many big Chinese cities have highly polluted air and water, and there are major concerns about food safety. Travel is a temporary release from these worries.
- **Education:** As more Chinese study abroad, and as their parents stay emotionally close to them, foreign vacations and business trips are built around spending time with offspring.
- **Real Estate and Investments:** Many Chinese with money believe that they have limited options to spend and park their wealth in China. This has given rise to a boom in overseas real estate and business investment by wealthy and near-wealthy Chinese. Many travel to purchase, work on, and enjoy these real estate and business investments.

Take a Walk on Boardwalk—Pass Go, Collect $200 (Thousand!)

The last reason is not something many have yet considered as a travel motivator. Paul Salo, an American expatriate in China with a colorful history—including making and losing fortunes, selling art as a destitute on the streets of China, and being kidnapped at gunpoint—finally found long-term success selling foreign real estate to Chinese families and investors.

Salo Homes has seen its business skyrocket over the past five years and, according to Salo, the reasons are "the need and desire to park liquid assets in foreign real estate, increased travel leading to better awareness of the global property market, and families looking to live bi-national lives." He predicts, "In the next five years, travel—influenced by the desire to purchase and the satisfaction in using real estate abroad—will triple."

Kevin Brown of Sotheby's has 25 years of experience selling property in New York, but in the last few years he has become something of a "Mr. China" for Manhattan real estate. He notes that Chinese consumers are the number-one foreign real estate buyers in New York

City, Los Angeles, Hawaii, and the Gold Coast of Long Island. "By far and away, the Chinese are the fastest-growing demographic we serve." His practice, one of the top five in Manhattan, reports that 35 percent of their sales are made to Chinese buyers, compared to a mere 5 percent just five years ago. That is how super consumers change industries, demographics, and company fortunes.

Regardless of motivation, it is beyond argument that Chinese travelers will be the most numerous, influential, and among the world's highest-spending travelers over the next five years. You need to make them a major part of your future, or be left behind by those who do.

Who will benefit from understanding how to identify, attract, serve, and retain Chinese travelers?

- Countries (small and large) who focus on Chinese travelers.
- Cities and states whose tourism boards actively engage China.
- Retailers.
- Luxury brands.
- Consumer product companies.
- Luxury service and experience providers.
- Hotels.
- Food and beverage companies.
- Sports franchises.
- Airlines.
- Resorts.

So where are Chinese travelers going? We have conducted our own research and pored over the research of dozens of other travel agencies, online travel sites, consultancies, industry groups, and others. While we hoped to provide a top-10, -20, or -30 list of destinations for travel and business, we found that it would be impossible.

There are easily 50 different credible top-20 lists for 2014. There was a huge variation in data collected, the methods of collection, the differentials between most visited, most desired, Asia versus non-Asia trips, and perceptions regarding what counts as a foreign trip or not. There is also the fact that the top destination lists change often based on current trends, politics, business environment, and investment opportunities. For instance, 18 months ago, Japan was a nonfactor, but because of a weak yen and an interest in Japan it has become a top-five destination on many lists.

We can, however provide you a list of destinations in composite form. These are the places Chinese travelers are going, love going to, and want to go to. It is where they are spending money, experiencing other cultures, relaxing, and engaging in business.

Asia–Oceania

- **Hong Kong:** Easy access, unique lifestyle, real estate, business, and shopping all draw.
- **Taiwan:** Closer ties than anytime since 1949, Mandarin speaking, cosmopolitan, and a different kind of Chinese culture.
- **Sydney/Australia:** Sun, beaches, business opportunities, and educational opportunities have made Australia a key destination.
- **Maldives:** Became a top destination after word of mouth of how Chinese tourists are catered to spread.
- **Japan:** Disregarding political tensions with China, Japan's standard of living, shopping, technology, and business opportunities propel it to a top spot.

Europe

- **Paris:** Feeds into the desire for culture, history, luxury, and shopping.
- **Rome:** For many of the same reasons that Paris is a draw.
- **London:** London was slow to realize the potential of Chinese travelers but is catching up. Heritage, history, and Burberry have improved London's ranking.

North America

- **New York City:** Far and away the top destination in North America for all of the same reasons Americans and foreigners alike love it. Shopping, fast pace, luxury, landmarks, history, media, and pop culture.
- **Las Vegas:** While Macao is still the top gambling destination for the Chinese, Las Vegas draws for its shows, proximity to the Grand Canyon, shopping, and the appeal of the Western life.
- **Los Angeles:** For the same reasons everyone loves L.A.—sunshine, beaches, celebrities, and luxury.

Up and Comers

- **Dubai:** Chinese tourists and business travelers have discovered the desert playground. There is something to the idea that it is Shanghai, Las Vegas, and Hong Kong rolled into one.
- **Bali:** A combination of resorts, a reputation for safety, natural beauty, and clean air appeal.
- **Phuket:** See Bali.

As Sage Brennan puts it, "Brands should take advantage of Chinese consumers' newfound obsession with travel to communicate and showcase their brand heritage and culture in ways that are not possible in China. Chinese consumers are hungry to learn and experience history and heritage and understand brand quality and workmanship. Utilize these assets to give your customers a truly unique experience that they cannot get in China. They will love your brand all the more for it, and reward you with higher spending across the globe."

This is true of any of the products and services mentioned above.

To truly benefit from the Chinese travel boom, you must strategize around three key imperatives:

1. **There are many levels of experience and sophistication among Chinese travelers.** There is no one-size-fits-all approach. People who have been traveling for business and pleasure for 10 years, newer travelers with two years of experience and a daughter at NYU, and one of the tens of millions making their first trips have different desires and needs. Figure out where you fit among them and tailor your bi-national approach to the right segment(s).

2. **Chinese travelers are people.** Christine Lu says, "Somewhere along the way, in the last five years, brands and companies that serve Chinese travelers and consumers went from not knowing they exist to treating them like walking dollar signs. My Chinese friends notice it. The worst thing you can do is treat them this way; they know what you are up to."

3. **Experiences matter.** Setting and experience are more important than ever. Whether you are selling couture dress, a luxury suite, or a fine meal, know that experience beyond the material matters.

THE TRUTH ABOUT CHINA'S RUDE TOURISTS

There was a lot of talk in the media in 2013 and 2014 about rude Chinese tourists. In some ways there is a parallel to the American super consumer of the 1950s and 1960s, who—when he began to travel abroad—developed a reputation as the ugly American, the loud, garish-clothes-wearing stereotype who was viewed by locals the world over as culturally, gastronomically, and linguistically barbaric.

Recent examples, which have sparked a firestorm of commentary in both Chinese and Western media, include a group of snorkelers who caught and ate endangered sea creatures off the Paracel Islands; visitors to North Korea who threw candy at North Korean children as if they were feeding ducks; swimmers who took pictures with a dying dolphin; and a teenage boy from Nanjing who scratched graffiti on a 3,000-year-old relic while touring Egypt with his parents.

In response, Chinese officials are making a concerted effort to improve the behavior of Chinese travelers abroad. In fact, they have issued a list of guidelines that include "no spitting, cutting lines, or taking your shoes and socks off in public." Vice Premier Wang Yang has stated that "improving the civilized quality of the citizens" is necessary for "building a good image" for the country.

Like many commentators, we are not convinced that Chinese travelers on the whole behave worse than other groups when abroad. We Yanks, along with our German and English friends, have long suffered poor reputations—somewhat deserved—as poor travelers.

Questions over whether the actions that the Chinese government is addressing are actually a widespread problem have already been discussed at length, to no avail. To us, there is a deeper lesson to be learned from the story—one in which brands, retailers, and service providers from around the world can capitalize.

The lesson is: While the media likes to sensationalize a few isolated incidents of bad behavior, there are obviously far more Chinese travelers interested in learning how to have the most sophisticated experience they can find. With tens of millions of newly wealthy travelers leaving the country every year, companies have the opportunity to expose China's new world citizens to local foods, beverages, fashion, hospitality, and experiences they may not have had.

It is important to remember that many of these Chinese business and pleasure travelers have little or no experience in international travel. This may lead to cultural misunderstandings, but it is also an opportunity for luxury companies to play a vital role in educating travelers about the best their brands have to offer.

Any traveler is curious about the world and wants to see and feel the places they have seen on TV, online, and at the movies. According to UN statistics, Chinese travelers particularly want to spend a lot of money while doing it: In 2005, the UN said, "China ranked seventh in international tourism expenditure, and has since successively overtaken Italy, Japan, France, and the United Kingdom." By 2012, "China leaped to first place, surpassing both top spender Germany and second-largest spender the United States (both close to $84 billion in 2012)."

Chinese travelers from the emerging middle, upper, and wealthy classes are still very much in a phase of development where they are seeking instruction and cues on how to build their sense of identity and their personal brands, with tastes informed by a mix of Chinese and Western cultures, aesthetics, and lifestyles. Conspicuous consumption among Chinese tourists is increasingly losing ground to a new desire for sophisticated travel experiences. These consumers certainly don't fit the stereotype of the Chinese tourist lined up outside a luxury goods store—rather, they want to impart to others their newly found sophistication by the wines they drink, the new foods they have tried, the hotels and resorts they stay at, the niche brands they wear, and the special experiences in which they have engaged.

With close to 60 percent of Chinese luxury purchases taking place outside the mainland, smart luxury companies can and should take the opportunity to educate Chinese consumers on how to build an identity through their experiences in foreign travel. By doing so, they retain brand loyalty when the travelers return home. Some examples include:

- The cosmetics retailer who holds a special private event for Chinese luxury travelers in order to educate them on products, looks, how to shop smartly for cosmetics around the world, and how they can keep up the look at home by obtaining the same product locally.
- The hotel that holds special events or provides Chinese travelers with pre- or in-trip collateral material on food, wine, and local attractions, while subtly including live-, look-, and act-like-a-local messaging into their programs. These extra touches may be the deciding factor for Chinese travelers choosing one five-star location over another, both domestically and abroad.
- The high-end fishing and wildlife excursion company in Alaska that gives Chinese consumers a sense of place and custom by providing

general and culture-specific lessons about the local ecology and land-scape (in addition to providing a luxury lodge, great meals, and superb fishing).

Chinese travelers carry the same needs and desires on the road as they have at home. Companies can build their brand, sell products and services, and retain customers by tapping into these needs and desires. And, at the same time, they can round out the travel experience with a life experience and an education in global sophistication.

■ ■ ■

Perhaps no facet of the current power of Chinese super consumers is more representative of the whole than the travel and tourism explosion. There is nothing more expressive of middle-class success and luxury living than travel.

China's super consumers are exhibiting their tastes, sophistication, spending power, adoption of the best of the West, and their ultimate Chineseness through travel. All of the industries, companies, and nations that stand to benefit from Chinese mass consumption find these benefits at their doorstep when China travels.

Consumer products, gifts, real estate, education, fashion, food and beverage, hotels, airlines, amusement parks. Business deals, relationship building, self expression, absorbing culture. Asserting the strength and wealth of China. All of this is expressed on the road and is a result of what is happening in China proper. The China market and the China global demographic have coupled and given birth to the Chinese super consumer. The question for you, your brand, your company, your future is: How can I help China grow, boost my bottom line, help my company and country profit, and do good while doing well? If you don't have a plan, you need one, and if you have one you must revisit it often.

Chinese super consumers have changed the world and will continue to change the world. You, your brand, your company must plan, adapt, improvise, and overcome the challenges presented by these facts to stay relevant and succeed in the next 20 years and beyond.

CHAPTER 21

Chinese Super Consumers Changing the World

Change is the law of life. And those who look only to the past or present are certain to miss the future.

—John F. Kennedy

American super consumers changed America and the world in the second half of the twentieth century. The same thing is happening in China today, in ways both subtle and profound, and anyone who is looking to the world's largest country as a potential market for goods and services needs to be aware of the massive shifts that are happening there.

At the beginning of this book, we wrote that it isn't a how-to guide for doing business in China. Rather, our real goal is to provide some context for what might well be the most important economic development going on in the world today.

The Microsoft Miracle

Let's look at what this all looks like in the real world. A lot of Western pundits have written off Microsoft as yesterday's news, but in China the world's largest software company (still) has been able to accomplish what few other companies have—and it all comes back to Microsoft's ability to identify, reach, and sell to super consumers.

Of all the major American Internet players—Google, Facebook, Twitter, Amazon.com, Apple, and Microsoft—it is Microsoft that has managed to most effectively overcome specific hurdles and integrate itself into the fabric of China's Internet and high-tech infrastructure. Specifically, Microsoft has deftly navigated both the government's significant presence in Chinese high-tech as well as the Chinese super consumer's ambivalence to software as a point-of-sale unit purchase.

Dr. Zhang Yaqin, chairman of Microsoft Asia Pacific Research and Development, is a world-renowned expert in digital imaging and audio, data compression and video, multimedia communications, and Internet technologies. A holder of 60 American patents, he joined Microsoft in 1999 and has been integral to the company's success in China.

"Back when I joined Microsoft 15 years ago, China was a country with the potential to become the number-one buyer in many categories," Dr. Zhang says. "Today China is the number-one market for personal computers, the largest wireless phone market, the largest automotive market, and is number one or two for many other products. So during the last 15 years the potential has become reality."

But China's rise as the world's top technology market has not included software. Dr. Zhang explains why: "For the IT market, China is very consumer-driven," continued Dr. Zhang. "In the United States, it is, first and foremost, enterprise-driven and then consumers. In China, it is very consumer-centric with both PC and mobile, and it is not likely to change in the future."

According to Dr. Zhang, a product like software, which a consumer cannot see or touch, does not penetrate a Chinese mind-set that values visible prestige, visual beauty, and obvious craftsmanship.

Until recently, software's tangible manifestation came in the form a disk, and the Chinese consumer simply could not justify paying hundreds or thousands of dollars for invisible code. Also, its value as intellectual property was not on the government's radar—thus its ambivalence toward piracy—although this has started to change.

Chinese consumers are much more open to the idea of paying for software as a cloud-based subscription service (SaaS), much the same way they would purchase magazines. Alibaba and Tencent (China's largest

Internet companies) are both based on the SaaS model and Microsoft has been an early mover, as well.

"The Chinese consumer has changed the dynamics of the software industry in China," Dr. Zhang says. "In the United States, software has been a multibillion dollar industry with applications like Microsoft Office and later with the advent of the Internet, software-as-a-service (SAAS) has become very popular and therefore companies use software-as-a-service from the Internet cloud. China has leapfrogged the software product industry and right into the software-as-a-service industry."

He adds that, "Chinese gaming companies actually make money from selling virtual goods, ads, and subscriptions. In America, consumers will pay 50 dollars to buy a software game in a box, CD, or cartridge. In China, many of the games are free but you pay for the usage or they are subsidized by the advertisers. People pay for the computer hardware, in some cases more expensive than in the United States, and they will pay for the software as a service to use it, just not for the software products."

In late 2012, Microsoft became the first major U.S. provider to launch a public cloud in China. It did so by licensing the technical know-how and rights to run Shanghai's municipal government in order to offer Office 365. Windows Azure began to roll out in China in 2013 through Chinese partner 21Vianet Group, a large, carrier-neutral, Internet data-services provider. Forrester, an American market research company, predicts that China's public cloud market volume will reach $3.8 billion by 2020.

Dr. Zhang also emphasizes Microsoft China's role in helping start-up companies by leveraging its cloud services. It has even set up floors in buildings in Beijing and Shanghai for start-ups that use Windows Azure as their accelerators.

"So far we have hosted at least 40 companies that don't need to spend resources on infrastructure or hardware," Dr. Zhang says. "They are using our cloud services without buying any computer servers. They graduate in six months and many of them become successful because we have helped them lower their costs and increase the speed of operations."

Another major milestone for Microsoft China is the recent lifting of the government's ban on sales of Microsoft's XBox One (and all other gaming platforms) gaming console. China is the world's top video-gaming market, but the country implemented a ban on video game consoles in 2000 after the government cited concerns about harmful effects that violent video games might have on the country's youth. The measure's relaxation will allow foreign-invested enterprises to ship their products into the country from factories in Shanghai's new free-trade zone (opened in 2014). Sony, Microsoft, and Nintendo will have an opportunity to stake a claim in this potentially massive market.

Microsoft China is the first foreign company to open up in Shanghai's Free Trade Zone. It invested in a joint venture with the Chinese TV company BesTV, a subsidiary of Shanghai Media Group, with a $237 million investment.

The key to Microsoft's success has been Dr. Zhang's diligent effort to study and understand the nuances of Chinese consumers and government structure, and the many different ways they both impact business. "The Chinese government is much more involved and plays a more active role with business than most other governments, so you have to fully understand clearly their policies and their national priorities," Dr. Zhang says. "I study all the documents and policies from the National People's Congress, and I pay close attention to the macro policies and how they relate to our industry."

He adds, "If you want to succeed, you need to align your priorities with the government policies to create a win–win. In China, Microsoft is a Chinese company and that is critical to our success here. For most foreign multinationals, they tend to go into two extremes. One extreme is they pay little or no attention to the Chinese government and they simply transplant their systems and business models to China without any modifications and think it will work accordingly.

"In most cases they failed because you just could not do that without adapting sufficiently to Chinese culture and policies. The other extreme is they pay too much attention to the government—they spent too much time and resources on local government and central government—so they become so receptive and compliant to the Chinese government that they are not paying enough attention to the market. China is actually very market-driven, so you must pay attention to the consumers; so it is a delicate balance. At the end of the day, the business cannot just depend on government, so you cannot say, 'I know the mayor or the governor so well, my business will do well.'"

Here we have to come to a point not previously mentioned in this book, but one that must also be a guiding principle for all companies selling to China's super consumers. That is: The policies and regulations in China, as well as the intimate bond between business and government, are at the heart of the super-consumer revolution. The government set the framework for a consumption economy, and is working daily to increase consumption as a percentage of GDP. Your goals, aims, strategies, and plans must align with the hopes and dreams of the Chinese government as much as the hopes and dreams of Chinese consumers. The China dream belongs to the Chinese people but is being midwifed by the central government.

The story of Amway, the US-based, direct-selling pioneer and market leader, tells the tale. They established operations in China in 1995, based on their US model of direct selling, but a 1998 government ban on direct selling in China confined the company to selling through stores, which was antithetical to their business model and they had no experience in it. Essentially Amway seemed to be dead in the water in China. After years of negotiations and relationship building, and compromise with numerous government agencies and officials, China loosened its rules on direct selling and allowed Amway to operate on a fusion store-based/direct-sales model, and soon after Amway relaunched. In 2008, China became Amway's number-one global market and revenue generator. Recognizing the market opportunity presented by China's super consumers, studying their needs and wants, engaging them directly, and working with the government led to Amway's success and is a good model for almost any business hoping to succeed in China.

A Final Word about China's Super Consumers

Some refer to the past 30 years as the Chinese Miracle. That is a reductive and patronizing view. The rise of China, while not inevitable, has not been a miracle; rather, it was the result of hard work, brave decisions, constant debate, experimentation, and self-examination. It had its foundations in thousands of years of accomplishments; it was good strategic planning followed by (mostly) good execution. China did not so much become a world changer as much as it reemerged as one.

The production economy helped urbanize and enrich hundreds of millions of Chinese citizens, and the consumption economy is changing as many, if not more, lives in China. Equally important is that super consumers are not only changing China, but changing the world. Like the explosion of American consumption in the past, there are positive changes and negative changes, there are winners and losers, and there is every multitude of reality, implication, and potential for good or bad in China's consumer boom as there was in America's and Europe's.

While there are most certainly some bad effects from the rise of the Chinese super consumer, we believe that the overall result is positive for both China and the world. We have addressed most of these positive effects and the ways in which they are changing Chinese people, businesses, and the country in general, but it is worth looking at a few macro changes and the opportunities and challenges ahead.

We have long held as our guiding principle *to do good while doing well*, as we live, do business, and work with and among the Chinese people. It is just as important to ensure that you are improving people's lives and the places they live as it is to make a profit, and doing the former, especially in China, can lead to the latter. This is an important point to remember for its altruistic as well as commercial implications.

The big vitamin and supplement company NBTY is a prime example. Chinese consumers have an insatiable desire for safe, foreign made vitamins and supplements. NBTY has brought more than 300 products to China that provide healthy and safe enhancements to Chinese consumers' diet. As a result China has become the company's number-two wholesale market in the world. In the United States, NBTY supports many local charities. Consistent with NBTY's corporate giving philosophy, NBTY and China Soong Ching Ling Foundation (CSCLF) have jointly set up the "CSCLF-NBTY Children Care Fund," which will make a multimillion RMB donation within five years to improve the nutrition of preschool children in China's eastern and Western areas.

"Supporting the China Soong Ching Ling Foundation is very consistent with the NBTY brand and what we want to be recognized for, and we want to be involved with an organization that is very influential and has a very positive reputation. That is the corporate image we want to project to China and Chinese consumers," said Jeffrey Nagel, chief executive.

We have worked for more than 20 years to build not only bridges between foreign and Chinese companies and executives, but to build cultural, linguistic, and personal ties between China and the rest of the world. Part of that process now includes understanding the good, the bad, and the ugly realities that China's super consumers have created in order to ensure the future growth and comfort of China and the foreign and domestic companies who have benefited and seek to continue benefiting from Chinese mass consumption. Opportunities and challenges are found in all three.

China's super consumers have changed the world we live in and will continue to do so in the coming years and decades. The largest and most important consumer class since postwar America will play an important part in how brands are established and marketed, how retail is conducted, how we use and benefit from technology, and what the global business and commercial landscape of the twenty-first century will look like.

We think it will look very much like the Chinese woman we described starting her day in the Shanghai Starbucks. The question you have to ask yourself is: Will I benefit from or be a victim of the Chinese super consumer boom?

■ ■ ■

We hope you found many answers and the spark for you to ask more questions in regard to who Chinese super consumers are; how they think; what is important to them, and what, where, when, and how they buy.

In parting we offer you a list of actions you can take in the short, middle, and long terms to start, expand, and improve your engagement with Chinese consumers. It is important that you have numerous people and departments working within your organization as well as key experts outside of it working together to set and execute your Chinese consumer strategy. These are a good start.

Short Term:

- Immerse yourself further in the information that will continue to enhance your understanding of Chinese history, culture, language, and mind-set to better understand Chinese consumers, purchase motivators, and the landscape you are operating in.
- Absorb as much current and topical information and news about China as you can. In a market that changes and grows this fast, today's realities and assumptions are tomorrow's failures if you are not careful.

- If you are planning to start engaging or to continue engaging Chinese consumers, repeat the daily mantras of: "strategy before structure" and "due diligence, due diligence, due diligence."

Short to Mid Term:

- Remember that China is not a monolith—it is a continental-size country with 1/6 of humanity living inside its borders. Make continental-sized plans for operations, sales, marketing, and delivery.
- Remember that China's super consumers are now everywhere in China. You can just as easily succeed selling $3 tubes of toothpaste in the hinterlands as you can selling $900 smartphones in the capitals.
- Use the above two points to deploy inside and outside resources that will provide the research, strategy, ability to execute, and ability to adjust.
- Remember that there is now a China global demographic as well as a China market(s). Integrate your services, infrastructure, brand experience, marketing, and sales to capture Chinese where they ARE spending, not where you want or think they are spending.
- Develop a Plan A and a Plan B for e-commerce, social media, and digital engagement, especially on mobile platforms as this is where engagement, peer recommendations, and sales are increasing.

Long Term:

- Build a long-term, heartfelt, and sincere relationship with Chinese consumers. They are not moving dollar signs; they are not Westerners because they carry iPhones and drive BMWs; they *will* see through your surface veneer if you do not offer substance and the promise of a mutually beneficial engagement.
- Cultivate relationships with the new generation of business leaders, academics, political leaders, and entrepreneurs inside and outside China. They are the generation of the one-child policy and they are well educated, sophisticated, English speaking, and ambitious. Aligning your business interests and purchasing desires is critical. Remember the average luxury consumer in China is 39 as opposed to 59 in the West.
- Be patient. Business, branding, and selling in China happen on China time, not yours. Imagine if you woke up one day and suddenly there

were 20, 50, 100 Chinese brands and retailers lining the main shopping street of your town or city. How many would you have an instant desire to engage with? How many would you trust? How many would you choose over the local brands you have been buying from for 10, 20, 30 years?

- Be patient again. It can take up to two years to get a proper read on how you are doing in China and with the China global demographic and 3-5 years to be truly profitable. In China patience is not just a virtue, but THE virtue.

INDEX

A

Advertising, 155–156
Affinity China, 111, 180–181
Affluent consumers, 149–150
Affordable-luxury sector, 183–186
Age of Discovery, 44, 45, 50
Age of Exploration, 42
Aging population, 151–152
Agriculture, 37, 58, 66, 122
Agriculture Industry Commerce
      Association (AIC), 94
Alcohol consumption, 9
Alibaba, 125, 130–132, 204–205
Ali Pay, 132
Ali Wang Wang, 132
Amazon, 131, 132, 204
American brands, 183, 185
American Century, 80–85
American Dream, 3, 6, 83–85, 118
American products, preference for,
    135
Americans, individualism of, 173
Amsterdam: The Story of the World's
    Most Liberal City (Shorto), 50
Amway, 207
Ancestor worship, 38
Annan, Kofi, 41
Anticorruption drives, 107
Apparel, 18, 70, 71, 118, 127, 140,
    151, 164–168
Apple, 204
Appliance market, 95–96, 163
Asia, as Chinese travel destination, 197

Audi, 8
Australia, 197

B

Baccardi, 172
Badge brands, 108
Bali, 198
Bang & Olufson, 185
Barry, Max, 53
Baskin-Robbins, 18
Baudelaire, Charles, 49
BDA China, 69
Beard, Mary Ritter, 191
Bedding, 31
Beer, 9
Beijing:
   Galleries Lafayette in, 127
   Lenovo in, 157
   as part of Coastal China, 8, 92
   retail outlets in, 18
   7-Eleven in, 121
Beijing Olympics, 73, 74
Beijing Snowflake, 96
Belstaff, 185
Best Buy, 127
BesTV, 206
Biederman, Paul, 191
Billboards, 155
Billionaires, 9
BMW, 183
Bohai Bay, 8
Boston Consulting Group, 135,
    163

Brands:
  in broadcast media, 172
  in department stores, 115
  and travel, 198
Brand advertising, 169–170
Brand halo effect, 150
Brennan, Sage, 69–70, 72–75, 188,
    198
Brian, Wei, 161–164
BRICS nations, 9, 19
British Empire, 34, 53–55
Broadcast media, 170–173
Brooks Brothers, 182–183
Brown, Kevin, 195–196
Buddhism, 38
Bush, George W., 85
Business culture, Chinese vs. Western
    approaches to, 27
Business strategy, 144–145
Business travel, 194
Buying, in supply chain, 142

C

Candles, 22
Canton, 86. *See also* Guangzhou
Canton Fair, 130
Car culture, 74–75, 82
Carmosky, Janet, 19, 25, 26
Car ownership, 17
Carrefour, 137
Castro, Fidel, 64
CBRE Research China, 114, 118
CGDM (China Global Demographic
    Market), 103–111
Chanel, 9, 170
Changchun-Harbin, 151
Changzhou, 92
Channels, 113–127. *See also*
    e-commerce
  China Post/Post Mart, 121–126
  convenience stores, 120–121
  department stores, 114–115
  grocery stores and supermarkets,
    118–119

  hypermarkets, 119–120
  lifestyle stores, 126–127
  malls, 116–118
  multibrand retail, 127
  specialty retailers, 127
  street-level stores, 115–116
Chen, Frank, 114
Chengdu, 121, 182
Chen Yi, 162
Cheung Kong Graduate School of
    Business (CKSB), 177
Chiang Kai Shek, 86
Chi ku, 186
China:
  contradictions in modern, 30–31
  as historical superpower, 13–14, 16
  learning about, 21–24, 209–210
  as market, 91–92
  population of, 7–8
  as self-contained empire, 33–39
  unique quality of growth in, 18–20
China Central Television (CCTV),
    155, 167, 172
The China Dream (Liu Mingfu), 3
"China-fy," 96, 98, 100
China Global Demographic, 103–111,
    157, 210
China Global Demographic Market
    (CGDM), 103–111
China Horizon Investment Group,
    121, 124–125
China Law Blog, 136
China Luxury Advisors, 70, 73–74,
    188
China Post, 121–126
China Resources Enterprise, 120
Chinese culture, 19, 21–32
  and Chinese mindset, 24–30
  importance of familiarity with,
    21–24
Chinese Dream, 118, 194
"The Chinese Dream," 3–6
Chinese language, 22, 23, 29, 37, 91,
    129

Chinese Miracle, 207
Chongqing, 121, 151
Chopard, 105
Chow Tai Fook, 116
City clusters, 150–151
Civil War, 86
Clingman, Alan, 121–125
Cloud computing, 204–205
Coach, 9, 116, 184, 187
Coastal China, 92
Coca-Cola, 22, 87, 94
Coffee, 9
Cold War, 81
Colgate-Palmolive, 87
Collectivization, 58
Colors, 23
Columbus, Christopher, 44, 45
Communists, 56, 86
Communist Party, 1, 2–3, 58
Confucianism, 38, 71
Confucius, 33
Conspicuous consumption, 200
Consumer boom, 71–75
Consumer culture, 16, 49–50
Consumerism, 70, 82
Convenience stores, 120–121
Converse, 127
Copyrights, 136
Corelle, 98
CorningWare, 98
Corruption, 107, 167, 186
Cosmetics, 162–163
Cost, total delivered, 141–142
Crusades, 41–42
Cuba, 64
Cultural Revolution, 59, 62–63
Culture, *see* Chinese culture
C-Wonder, 185

D

Dalian, 8
Daoism, 38
Decollectivization, 66
Delorme, 185

Deng Xiaoping, 1–2, 16, 63, 65–67,
      87, 117
Department stores, 98, 114–115
Detroit, Michigan, 82
Digital Mall, 132
Discretionary income, 156
Disposable income, 99–100, 149
Distribution, and supply chain,
      143–144
Distribution channels, *see* Channels
Domino's, 96–97
Dongguan, 8, 92
Dong Mingzhu, 163
Dubai, 198
Dutch East India Company, 50

E

East and West Designs, 26
East China Design and Energy
      Company for the
      Environment, 164
EBay, 131, 132
E-commerce, 129–138, 152, 153,
      168. *See also* Alibaba
Edelman, 134
Educational travel, 195
E! Entertainment Television, 170
Eisenhower, Dwight D., 82
Elliman, Douglas, 174
Emporio Armani, 183
Empress Dowager, 55, 59
English language, 29
eno footwear, 70
Entertainment, shopping as, 152
Environmental concerns, 195
Ermenegildo Zegna, 18, 87,
      140–141
Estée Lauder, 163
Etsy, 132
Europe, as Chinese travel destination,
      197
European Dream, 6
Europeans, 38, 44–45, 50
Export Now, 134–135

F

Facebook, 174, 204
Family Mart, 121
Fast moving consumer goods (FMCG),
    5, 87, 179
Federal Interstate Highway System, 82
FICEs (foreign invested corporate
    entities), 101
First Emperor, 36
First globalization, 41–42
FITs (fully independent travelers),
    193–194
Five-Year Plan (FYP), 3–4
FMCG, *see* Fast moving consumer
    goods
Focus Money magazine, 134
Ford, Henry, 16
Foreign invested corporate entities
    (FICEs), 101
Foreign real estate buyers, 195–196
Formosa, *see* Taiwan
Forrester Research, 130
Fortune, 163
Four Modernizations, 1
Fred Myer, 119
Freedom, 4–5
Free Trade Zone (Shanghai), 206
Fujian province, 8, 92
Fully independent travelers (FITs),
    193–194
Fuzhou, 8
Fuzhou-Xiamen, 151
FYP (Five-Year Plan), 3–4

G

Galleries Lafayette, 127
Gandhi, Mohandas, 21
Gang of Four, 62–63
Ganster, Steve, 93–95, 97–98, 101
Gates, Bill, 91
Gellman, Richard, 106–107
General Motors (GM), 8
Genghis Khan, 43
George III, King, 53

Germany, 83
Gernert, Douglas, 135
G.I. Bill, 81
Gifts, 36
Gifting, luxury, 181
Giordano, 18
Globalization:
    and China Global Demographic,
        103–111
    first, 41–42
Globalization 1.0, 15
Globalization 2.0, 15
GM (General Motors), 8
GM Building (New York), 163
Gome, 127
Google, 204
Gossip Girl, 171
Gotta-have-it mindset, 156
Goverment rules and regulations,
    113
Graff, Roy, 192–194
Great Depression, 81
Greater China, 35
Great Leap Forward, 59, 63
"The Great Pizza Wars," 96–97
GREE Electric Appliances, 163
Greek Empire, 35
Gretzky, Wayne, 97
Grocery stores, 118–119
Gross, Dave, 187, 188
Group dynamics, 27
Guangdong province, 92, 121
Guangxu, Prince, 55
Guangzhou, 94, 130, 133
    as city cluster, 151
    and colonial exploitation, 53–54
    as part of Coastal China, 8, 92
    Post Mart in, 124
Guanxi, 134, 186
Gucci, 9, 187

H

Häagen Dazs, 74
Haier, 96

Halo effect, brand, 150
Han Dynasty, 36
Han ethnic group, 61, 91
Hangzhou, 8, 92, 131, 166
Hao, Emma, 174–176
Harmonious Society, 3
Harris, Dan, 136
Harry Winston, 116
Hartmann, Renee, 69–75
Heilongjiang Province, 100
Heineken, 74
Hello Hollywood! (television show), 171
Henan province, 124
Hershey, 9
Hierarchies, 27
Hirohito, Emperor, 56
History, Chinese, 21–24, 209
H&M, 116, 184
Hollywood, 81
Home Depot, 127
Home Shopping Network (HSN), 161–163
Homonyms, 22, 29
Hongbao, 167, 186
Hong Kong:
    and colonial exploitation, 53, 54
    Emporio Armani in, 183
    Lenovo in, 157–158
    as part of Coastal China, 8, 92
    and Shenzhen, 66–67
    Technomic Consultants in, 94
    as tourist destination, 193
HSN (Home Shopping Network), 161–163
Hu, Mark, 95
Hua Guofeng, 65
Hua Hai Zhong Lu, 115–116
Hubei province, 161
Hublot, 116
Huizhou, 8
Hunan TV, 164
Husband daycares, 118
Hypermarkets, 119–120

I

IBM, 157–159
IGD, 118
Implementation, supply chain, 145
Impulse buying, 152
India, 64
Individualism, 173
Industrialization, 58–59
Ingrao, Tony, 175
Initial public offerings (IPOs), 131
Inner China, 36
Insider trading, 69
Intellectual property (IP), 136, 204
Internet, 205
Interstate Highway System, 82
Inventions, Chinese, 37–38, 49
IPOs (initial public offerings), 131
iQiyi, 171

J

Japan, 55–57, 67, 80, 83, 86, 196–197
JD.com, 135–137
Jerry Maguire (film), 93
Jiang Qing, 62–63
Jiangsu province, 8, 92
Jiangxi province, 124
Jiang Zemin, 2
Joint ventures, 94–95, 101
Joyce Beauty, 163

K

Kate Spade, 184
Kate Zhou Handbags, 116
Kennedy, John F., 203
KFC, 74
Kmart, 119
KMPG, 105
Korea, 80
Kraft, 87
Kublai Khan, 43–44
Kunming, 151
Kuomintang Party (KMT), 55, 86
Kutcher, Ashton, 159

L

Lancôme, 163
Land reform, 58
Lane Crawford, 116, 127
Las Vegas, Nevada, 197
Lavazza Coffee, 172
Lavin, Frank, 134
Lawson, 121
Lee, Ann, 85
Lee Jeans, 172
Lenovo, 157–161
Lew, Andy, 182–183
Liao Central South, 151
Lifestyle experience, travel as, 194–195
Lifestyle stores, 126–127
Li & Fung, 106
Li Ning, 116, 127
Literacy, 59
Liu Chuanzhi, 157, 158
Liu Mingfu, 3
London, England, 197
Longines, 105
L'Oréal, 163
Los Angeles, California, 197
Louis Vuitton, 9, 87, 185
Lu, Christine, 111, 180–181, 198
Luxury goods and brands, 179–189
    affordable-luxury sector, 183–186
    and corruption, 107
    downturn in, 186–189
    expansion of, 9, 14, 70, 74
    and gifting group, 181
    and middle-class consumers, 182–183
    and nouveau riche, 180–181
    Tourneau, 104–107
    and travel, 200
LVMH, 179

M

Ma, Jack, 130, 131
Macao, 54
McCartney, Lord George, 53
McDonald's, 74
McGregor, James, 14

McKinsey & Company, 9, 147–153
McKinsey Technology Institute, 148
Magnes Sisters, 116
Mainstream consumers, 149–150
Makeup, 79
Maldives, 197
Malls, 116–118
Manchuria, 56
Mandarin Chinese, 29, 129
Mandarins (civil servants), 16
Manufacturing, 67, 142–143
Maoism, 64
Mao Zedong, 2, 6, 57, 63
Market clusters, 92
Marketing, 155–178
    and brand advertising, 169–170
    and consumer impulses/desires, 156
    by Lenovo, 157–161
    and made for China TV, 170–173
    by O.C.T. Mami, 164–168
    via promotions, 177
    via social media, 173–177
    by WeiEast, 161–164
Market segmentation, 147–153
Markman, Scott, 156, 169–170
Marx, Karl, 71
Marxism, 64
Maternity wear, 164–168
Maurizi, Cynthia, 84
Maxim's, 18
Medicine, traditional, 37
Megaprocesses, supply chain, 140–141
Meiji Restoration, 55–56
Meitan Me You, 170
Melnitsky, Ira, 104–107
Metan Development, 170–173
Mexico, 143
Michael Kors, 184, 187
Microsoft, 203–207
Middle class, 114
    American, 81
    creation of, 4
    and luxury market, 182–183
Middle Kingdom, 34, 61

Mindset, Chinese, 24–30
Ming Dynasty, 36, 45–46
Ministop, 121
Mobile purchases, 137
Modern Life, 171
Mongols, 34
Mongolia, 35
The Monogram Group, 156
Morris, Ian, 37
Morrison, Van, 43
Multibranding, 72
Multibrand retail, 127
Musical instruments, 9

N

Nagel, Jeffrey, 208
Namer, Larry, 170–172
Nanjing, 8, 92, 151
Nanning, 151
National Basketball Association (NBA),
    133
National Football League (NFL),
    132–135
Nationalist government, 55
Nationalists, 56
NBA (National Basketball Association),
    133
NBTY, 208
Nestlé, 94, 100
Networks, 27–28
New China, 58–59
New World, 34, 50, 114
New York City, 197
NFL (National Football League),
    132–135
Nike, 18, 71–73, 127
Nike China, 70
99 Reforms, 55
Ningbo, 8, 92
Nintendo, 206
Nomads, 35
Nordstrom, 127
North America, as Chinese travel
    destination, 197

Nouveau riche, 180–181, 187
Novelty value, 152

O

Oceania, as Chinese travel destination,
    197
O.C.T. Mami, 164–168
Office 365 (software), 205
Ogilvy and Mather, 69
Olympic games, 73, 74
Omega, 105
One Billion Customers (McGregor),
    14
Online shopping, 134. *See also*
    e-commerce
Opening and Reform, 73, 193
Operations strategy, 144–145
Opium, 54
Opium War, 72
Orient (corporation), 114
Orr, Gordon, 147–153
Outbound China, 184–185

P

Paris, France, 197
Parkson, 114
Patek Phillip, 105
Patience, 210–211
PayPal, 132
Pearl River Delta, 8
Peer recommendations, 178
People's Republic, founding and early
    days of, 57–59, 87
Pepsi, 22, 87
Per-capita disposable income, 149
Personal computer market, 157–161
P&G, *see* Procter & Gamble
Pizza Hut, 96
Planet Homebuddies (Internet television
    series), 171
Planning, supply chain, 141–142
Pollution, 195
Polo, Maffeo, 43
Polo, Marco, 43–44

Polo, Niccolo, 43
Pompadur, Larry, 170
Porsche, 8
Ports (brand), 18
Post Mart, 123–125
PPTV, 171
Prada, 9, 179, 187
PricewaterhouseCoopers, 120
Problem solving, 28
Proclamation 13 (State Council),
    71, 73
Procter & Gamble (P&G), 87,
    94, 97
Promotions, 177
Pyrex, 98

Q

Qianlong, 53
Qingdao, 8, 54, 86, 121
Qing Dynasty, 34, 38, 54–55, 61,
    86–87

R

Ralph Lauren, 126, 185
Real estate, foreign, 195–196
Rebecca Minkoff, 116
"Red Computer," 160
Reform and Opening, 1, 22, 65–68,
    79, 165
Relationships, cultivating, 210
Renaissance, 42, 45
Returnees, 25
Return to Da Fu Tsun (television show),
    172
Roaring Twenties, 81
Rolex, 105, 116
Roman Empire, 35
Rome, Italy, 197
Roosevelt Island, 175
Rude Chinese tourists, 199
Rudin, Melanie, 106–107
Russia, Soviet, *see* Soviet Union
Russo-Japanese war, 55–56

S

Sales channels, *see* Channels
Salo, Paul, 195
Salo Homes, 195
"Scientific Development," 3
Segmentation, 147–153
Self-confidence, 38, 156
Self-expression, 28–30
Self-image, 24
Selling, in supply chain, 144
Senior market, 151
Sephora, 79–80, 116, 127, 163
Sequoia Capital, 168
7-Eleven, 120–121
SEZs (special economic zones), 66–67
Shaanxi province, 107
Shandong province, 124
Shanghai:
    as city cluster, 151
    and colonial exploitation, 54
    and Deng's Southern Tour, 117
    as first-tier city, 73
    Hua Hai Zhong Lu in, 115–116
    Microsoft in, 205, 206
    as part of Coastal China, 8, 92
    as "Pearl of the Orient," 86
    Post Mart in, 124
    retail outlets in, 18
    Sephora in, 79–80
    7-Eleven in, 121
    Tompkins International in, 140
Shanghai #1 Bedding store, 116
Shanghai Media Group, 206
Shanghai Plaza 66 (shopping mall),
    185
Shanghai Tang, 116, 184
Shenyang, 182
Shenzhen:
    as city cluster, 151
    Hong Kong investment in, 66–67
    multinationals and, 124
    as part of Coastal China, 8, 92
    retail outlets in, 18
    Whirlpool in, 95

Shopping:
  as entertainment, 152
  and travel, 194
Shorto, Russell, 50
Shuangcheng, 100
Silk Road, 42
Silk Road Era, 34
Sina Weibo, 171, 174
Skincare products, 162–163
Slogans, 1
Socialism with Chinese
     Characteristics, 1–2
Social media, marketing via,
    173–177
SOEs (state-owned enterprises), 121
Softbank, 130
Software, 204–205
Soho China, 163
Song Dynasty, 36, 37
Sony, 206
Sophisticated consumers, 126
Sotheby's, 195
Southern Tour, 87, 117
Soviet Union, 59, 62, 64, 80
SpaceNK, 163
Special Administrative Region,
    see Hong Kong
Special economic zones (SEZs),
    66–67
Specialty retailers, 127
Starbucks, 9, 18, 72–74
State Council, 71, 73
State-owned enterprises (SOEs),
    121
State-owned shops, 113
Staying the course, 98–100
Strategy, operations, 144–145
Street-level stores, 115–116
Structure, supply chain, 145
Subscription-as-a-service (SaaS),
    204–205
Sun Baohong, 67–68, 86, 177
Suning, 127
Sun Yat Sen, 55, 85

Super consumption:
  American, 81–82
  globalization of, 82–83
  origins of Chinese, 85–89
Supermarkets, 118–119
Supply chains, 139–145
  and alignment of strategy/structure/
      implementation, 144–145
  and buying, 142
  and distribution, 143–144
  and manufacturing, 142–143
  megaprocesses in, 140–141
  and planning, 141–142
  and selling, 144
Surplus Labor Value, 71
Suzhou, 8, 73, 92, 108, 124, 184
Sydney, Australia, 197

T

T-4 strategy (Whirlpool), 95
TAG Heuer, 105
Taiping Rebellion, 55
Taiwan, 35, 53, 165, 197
Tang Dynasty, 34, 36
"Tang" family, 107–111
Tao Bao, 125, 132, 137
Target, 119
Technology market, 204
Technomic Consultants, 93–94
Tencent, 174, 204–205
The Three Represents, 2–3
360buy.com, 135–136
Thrift, 36
Thunderbird School, 93
Tiangshan earthquake, 62–63
Tianjin, 8, 86
Tibet, 35
Tier-one cities, 70, 117, 124, 150, 151,
    182, 184
Tier-two cities, 70, 117, 124, 150, 182,
    184
Tiffany's, 183
Tingler, Brion, 158–161
Tmall, 132–135, 137

"Toddler" consumers, 99
"To get rich is glorious," 2, 67
Tompkins Asia, 5
Tompkins International, 139–140
Tompkins, Jim, 140
Tony Burch, 171, 187
Total delivered cost, 141–142
Totes Isotoner Corporation, 135
Tourneau, 104–107, 188
Trade, 35, 49–50, 71, 208
Trademarks, 136
Trade society, China as, 68
Traditional medicine, 37
Transportation, 143
Travel and tourism, 82, 191–201
　and brands, 198
　and China Global Demographic,
　　103–111
　destinations for, 196–198
　and foreign real estate buyers,
　　195–196
　increase in, 191–194
　key motivators for, 194–195
　rude Chinese tourists, 199
　strategizing tips for, 198, 200–201
Treaty Ports, 54–55
Tudou/Youku, 171
Tusk, 116
TV stations, 170–172
21Vianet Group, 205
Twitter, 174, 204
Two-Dollar-a-Day project (Procter &
　Gamble), 97

U

"Ugly American," 82
Unilever, 94
Uniqlo, 116
United Kingdom, 152
United States:
　and American Century, 80–85
　China as viewed by, 33–34
　as Chinese travel destination, 197
　population of, 8

University Flag Football League, 133
Urban, Pope, 41–42
Urbanization, 187–188
U.S. China Partners, 5
U.S. Postal Service, 125

V

Value consumers, 149–150
Value systems, Chinese vs. American/
　Western, 25–26
Vans (brand), 126–127
Video games, 205–206
Vitamins and supplements, 208

W

Walmart, 119, 137
Wanamaker, John, 155
Wang Xiuli, 124
War of Resistance, 57
WeChat, 106, 174–176
Wei East, 161–164
Wenxhoi, 92
What America Can Learn from China
　(Lee), 85
Whirlpool, 95–96
Wenzhou, 8
Wholly foreign owned enterprises
　(WOFEs), 101
Why the West Rules—for Now (Morris),
　37
Windows Azure, 205
Wine, 9
WOFEs (wholly foreign owned
　enterprises), 101
Women:
　fashion-conscious, 161, 166
　richest, 163–164
　status of, 59, 79
World Kitchen, 98
World Trade Organization (WTO), 2,
　38, 72–74, 191
World War II, 57, 80
Wuhan, 161
Wuxi, 8, 92

X

Xanadu, 43
XBox One, 205–206
Xiamen, 8
Xi'an, 25, 182
Xi Jinping, 1, 3–5, 107,
      186
Xinhai revolution, 55
Xinjiang, 35
Xiu.com, 137

Y

Yahoo!, 130
Yang Liu, 26, 29
Yangtze River, 36
"Yan Wu," 14–15, 17
Yellow River, 36
Yoga 2 tablet, 159

Yuan Dynasty, 34, 45, 61
Yum! brands, 87

Z

Zakkour, Hal, 84
Zakkour, Michael, 84–85
Zara, 116, 184
Zegna, 116
Zhang Ronglin, 124
Zhang Xin, 163
Zhang Yaqin, 204–206
Zhao, Paul, 164–168
Zhao Wenhong, 164
Zhejiang province, 8, 92, 165
Zheng He, 45–46
Zhou Enlai, 63
Zhu Di, 46–47
Zhu Rongji, 2